Modern Middle East Nations

AND THEIR STRATEGIC PLACE IN THE WORLD

IRAQ

Modern Middle East Nations
AND THEIR STRATEGIC PLACE IN THE WORLD

IRAQ

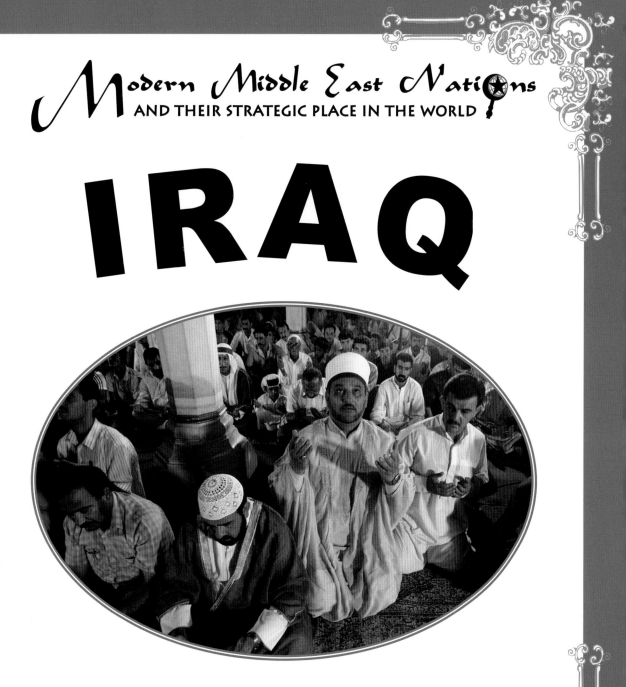

BILL AND DORCAS THOMPSON

MASON CREST PUBLISHERS
PHILADELPHIA

Produced by OTTN Publishing, Stockton, New Jersey

Mason Crest Publishers
370 Reed Road
Broomall, PA 19008
www.masoncrest.com

First printing

1 3 5 7 9 8 6 4 2

Library of Congress Cataloging-in-Publication Data

Thompson, William, 1931-
  Iraq / Bill and Dorcas Thompson.
      p. cm. — (Modern Middle East nations and their strategic place in the world)
Summary: Discusses the geography, history, economy, government, religion, people, foreign
relations, and major cities of Iraq.
Includes bibliographical references and index.
  ISBN 1-59084-508-0
  1. Iraq—Juvenile literature. [1. Iraq.] I. Thompson, Dorcas. II. Title. III. Series.
DS70.62 .T49 2003 956.7—dc21
                                                                        2002013000

Modern Middle East Nations
AND THEIR STRATEGIC PLACE IN THE WORLD

TABLE OF CONTENTS

Modern Middle East Nations

AND THEIR STRATEGIC PLACE IN THE WORLD

Dr. Harvey Sicherman, president and director of the Foreign Policy Research Institute, is the author of such books as *America the Vulnerable: Our Military Problems and How to Fix Them* (2002) and *Palestinian Autonomy, Self-Government and Peace* (1993).

Introduction

by Dr. Harvey Sicherman

Situated as it is between Africa, Europe, and the Far East, the Middle East has played a unique role in world history. Often described as the birthplace of religions (notably Judaism, Christianity, and Islam) and the cradle of civilizations (Egypt, Mesopotamia, Persia), this region and its peoples have given humanity some of its most precious possessions. At the same time, the Middle East has had more than its share of conflicts. The area is strewn with the ruins of fortifications and the cemeteries of combatants, not to speak of modern arsenals for war.

Today, more than ever, Americans are aware that events in the Middle East can affect our security and prosperity. The United States has a considerable military, political, and economic presence throughout much of the region. Developments there regularly find their way onto the front pages of our newspapers and the screens of our television sets.

Still, it is fair to say that most Middle Eastern countries remain a mystery, their cultures and religions barely known, their peoples and politics confusing and strange. The purpose of this book series is to change that, to educate the reader in the basic facts about the 23 states and many peoples that make up the region. (For our purpose, the Middle East also includes the North African states linked by ethnicity, language, and religion to the Arabs, as well as Somalia and Mauritania, which are African but share the Muslim religion and are members of the Arab League.) A notable feature of the series is the integration of geography, demography, and history; economics and politics; culture and religion. The careful student will learn much that he or she needs to know about ever so important lands.

A few general observations are in order as an introduction to the subject matter.

The first has to do with history and politics. The modern Middle East is full of ancient sites and peoples who trace their lineage and literature to antiquity. Many commentators also attribute the Middle East's political conflicts to grievances and rivalries from the distant past. While history is often invoked, the truth is that the modern Middle East political system dates only from the 1920s and was largely created by the British and the French, the victors of World War I. Such states as Algeria, Iraq, Israel, Jordan, Kuwait, Saudi Arabia, Syria, Turkey, and the United Arab Emirates did not exist before 1914—they became independent between 1920 and 1971. Others, such as Egypt and Iran, were dominated by outside powers until well after World War II. Before 1914, most of the region's states were either controlled by the Turkish-run Ottoman Empire or owed allegiance to the Ottoman sultan. (The sultan was also the caliph or highest religious authority in Islam, in the line of the prophet Muhammad's successors, according to the beliefs of the majority of Muslims known as the Sunni.) It was this imperial Muslim system that was ended by the largely British military victory over the Ottomans in World War I. Few of the leaders who emerged in the wake of this event were happy with the territories they were assigned or the borders, which were often drawn by Europeans. Yet, the system has endured despite many efforts to change it.

The second observation has to do with economics, demography, and natural resources. The Middle Eastern peoples live in a region of often dramatic geographical contrasts: vast parched deserts and high mountains, some with year-round snow; stone-hard volcanic rifts and lush semi-tropical valleys; extremely dry and extremely wet conditions, sometimes separated by only a few miles; large permanent rivers and wadis, riverbeds dry as a bone until winter rains send torrents of flood from the mountains to the sea. In ancient times, a very skilled agriculture made the Middle East the breadbasket of the Roman Empire, and its trade carried luxury fabrics, foods, and spices both East and West.

Most recently, however, the Middle East has become more known for a single commodity—oil, which is unevenly distributed and largely concentrated in the Persian Gulf and Arabian Peninsula (although large pockets are also to be found in Algeria, Libya, and other sites). There are also new, potentially lucrative offshore gas fields in the Eastern Mediterranean.

This uneven distribution of wealth has been compounded by demographics. Birth rates are very high, but the countries with the most oil are often lightly populated. Over the last decade, Middle East populations under the age of 20 have grown enormously. How will these young people be educated? Where will they work? The failure of most governments in the region to give their people skills and jobs (with notable exceptions such as Israel) has also contributed to large out-migrations. Many have gone to Europe; many others work in other Middle Eastern countries, supporting their families from afar.

Another unsettling situation is the heavy pressure both people and industry have put on vital resources. Chronic water shortages plague the region. Air quality, public sanitation, and health services in the big cities are also seriously overburdened. There are solutions to these problems, but they require a cooperative approach that is sorely lacking.

A third important observation is the role of religion in the Middle East. Americans, who take separation of church and state for granted, should know that most countries in the region either proclaim their countries to be Muslim or allow a very large role for that religion in public life. Among those with predominantly Muslim populations, Turkey alone describes itself as secular and prohibits avowedly religious parties in the political system. Lebanon was a Christian-dominated state, and Israel continues to be a Jewish state. While both strongly emphasize secular politics, religion plays an enormous role in culture, daily life, and legislation. It is also important to recall that Islamic law (*Sharia*) permits people to practice Judaism and Christianity in Muslim states but only as *Dhimmi*, protected but very second-class citizens.

Fourth, the American student of the modern Middle East will be impressed by the varieties of one-man, centralized rule, very unlike the workings of Western democracies. There are monarchies, some with traditional methods of consultation for tribal elders and even ordinary citizens, in Saudi Arabia and many Gulf States; kings with limited but still important parliaments (such as in Jordan and

Morocco); and military and civilian dictatorships, some (such as Syria) even operating on the hereditary principle (Hafez al Assad's son Bashar succeeded him). Turkey is a practicing democracy, although a special role is given to the military that limits what any government can do. Israel operates the freest democracy, albeit constricted by emergency regulations (such as military censorship) due to the Arab-Israeli conflict.

In conclusion, the MODERN MIDDLE EAST NATIONS series will engage imagination and interest simply because it covers an area of such great importance to the United States. Americans may be relative latecomers to the affairs of this region, but our involvement there will endure. We at the Foreign Policy Research Institute hope that these books will kindle a lifelong interest in the fascinating and significant Middle East.

Smoke rises from one of Saddam Hussein's presidential palaces in Baghdad following a U.S. air strike, March 31, 2003. American and British military action finally dislodged the Iraqi dictator after nearly a quarter century in power.

Place in the World

In the early-morning hours of March 20, 2003, U.S. bombs and cruise missiles slammed into a concrete bunker in the southern part of Baghdad, the capital city of Iraq. The target of the attack was Iraq's dictator, Saddam Hussein, who had defied the United Nations and the West for more than a decade, refusing to comply with a series of requirements the international community had imposed on his defeated country after the 1991 Gulf War. In particular, Saddam had skirted Iraq's obligation to account for, and give up, certain classes of offensive weapons. The March attack, which marked the start of a second gulf war, came after months of escalating tensions between the United States and Iraq.

During the 1980s the United States had given military and financial support to Saddam Hussein's government, but the relationship turned sour after Iraq invaded its tiny neighbor Kuwait in August 1990. To oppose Iraq's aggression, the

United States took the lead in building an international military coalition of more than 30 countries, and the United Nations demanded that Iraq withdraw its forces from Kuwait by January 15, 1991. The day after this deadline had passed with Iraqi troops still in Kuwait, Operation Desert Storm began with a campaign of aerial bombardment. After coalition warplanes bombed strategic targets in Iraq and Kuwait for several weeks, a multinational ground force, composed mainly of U.S. and British troops, moved in and quickly routed the Iraqi army. By the end of February, Iraqi soldiers were fleeing Kuwait, although hundreds were killed along a stretch of road between the two countries that became known as the "highway of death." On February 28, 1991, with the goal of liberating Kuwait achieved, the United States unilaterally declared a cease-fire.

A television image shows two victims of Iraq's chemical-weapons attack on the Kurdish village of Halabja. The March 1988 atrocity, which claimed the lives of about 5,000 Kurds, came near the end of Iraq's eight-year-long war with Iran.

As wars go, the 1991 Gulf War was relatively short. However, in many respects the peace that followed was more problematic. Throughout his rule Saddam Hussein had actively promoted the development of weapons of mass destruction—a term that refers to chemical, biological, and nuclear weapons. During a war with Iran (1980–88), Iraq's non-Arab neighbor to the east, Saddam's forces had used chemical weapons such as mustard gas (a vesicant that burns and blisters the skin, eyes, and respiratory tract) and sarin (a nerve agent that causes convulsions and death by paralysis of the respiratory tract). Saddam also ordered the use of chemical weapons against Iraq's Kurdish minority. The most infamous attack, in March 1988, left some 5,000 people dead in the Kurdish village of Halabja. Iraqi military scientists had been developing biological agents such as anthrax, which when inhaled causes severe, often fatal, respiratory problems. In addition, Saddam had been working since the mid-1970s to acquire nuclear weapons. Experts believe that by 1991 Iraq was just a few years away from becoming a nuclear power.

RESOLUTIONS, INSPECTIONS, AND SANCTIONS

After the end of the 1991 Gulf War, the United Nations Security Council passed a number of resolutions, which set out the conditions for peace. Resolution 686 (adopted March 2, 1991) declared a cease-fire in the Gulf War. In return, Iraq was ordered to recognize Kuwait's sovereignty, return Kuwaiti property and account for Kuwaiti prisoners, end support of terrorism, and pay damages for its invasion of Kuwait. Resolution 687 (April 3, 1991) ordered Iraq to stop building weapons of mass destruction and to destroy those it already possessed. The disarmament was to be done within 105 days. The United Nations established a special commission, UNSCOM, to oversee the disarming of Iraq. Inspection teams sent by UNSCOM were supposed to be given "immediate, unconditional, and unrestricted" access to any buildings, vehicles, equipment, or records the teams wished to examine.

U.N. Security Council Resolution 688 (April 5, 1991) condemned Saddam's efforts to put down a revolt by Iraq's Kurdish civilians. U.S. and British fighter jets started to patrol a "no-fly zone" in the northern part of the country, through which Iraqi warplanes were not permitted to fly. This was intended to protect the Kurds from attack. The next year a second no-fly zone was set up in the southern part of the country, where Iraq's Shiite Muslim population was concentrated, after Saddam had tried to repress Shiite dissidents who opposed his rule.

Over the next decade, however, Saddam and his government frustrated the efforts of UNSCOM inspection teams. In August 1991 the U.N. Security Council passed Resolution 707, which condemned Iraq's "serious violation" of Resolution 687 and its noncompliance with the Nuclear Non-Proliferation Treaty. Ten more U.N. resolutions would have similar wording, culminating with Resolution 1205 (November 5, 1998), which condemned "the decision by Iraq of 31 August 1998 to cease cooperation with" UNSCOM inspectors.

Despite the lack of cooperation from Iraqi leaders, the UNSCOM inspectors oversaw the destruction of much of Saddam Hussein's stocks of chemical and biological agents. However, some of the inspectors believed there were areas of the country that they had not been permitted to inspect, where banned weapons might still exist.

On December 16, 1998, after the U.N. weapons inspectors withdrew from Baghdad, the United States launched air strikes against Iraq. In an address from the White House, President Bill Clinton explained that the strikes were intended to send a message to Saddam Hussein: "If you act recklessly, you will pay a heavy price." The air strikes soon ended, but the U.N. weapons inspectors would not be permitted to return to Iraq for four years.

Throughout the 1990s and early 2000s, the international community also tried to pressure Iraq to disarm through economic sanctions, which had been put in place before the 1991 Gulf War. However, the sanctions had only limited success. As dictator of Iraq, Saddam Hussein exercised great control over the country's economy. Not only did he use his power to enrich himself—building a personal fortune valued at more than $7 billion—but he was also able to allocate a great proportion of his nation's resources to military projects.

At the same time, many Iraqis faced starvation, medical problems, and shortages of essential items. To alleviate the suffering of Iraq's people, the United Nations in the mid-1990s started a program that permitted Iraq to sell its oil in exchange for food, medicine, and other goods necessary for its citizens.

Some people criticized the "oil-for-food" program, saying the money brought in by Iraq's sale of oil helped Saddam's regime remain in power, rather than helping ordinary Iraqis. Others criticized the U.N. sanctions, seeing them as the cause of much suffering among the Iraqi people. However, defenders of the program noted that the economic sanctions did not prohibit food, medicine, or humanitarian aid. They also pointed out that Saddam had not even agreed to participate in the "oil-for-food" program for more than 18 months after it was initially proposed by the United Nations, and that he did not use the money from the oil sales to alleviate his people's suffering.

The United States and other nations did not want to go to war with Iraq again. During the 1990s the nations of the West followed a policy of "containment"—the idea being that patrolling the no-fly zones over northern and southern Iraq, enforcing the sanctions, and supporting the efforts of UNSCOM inspectors would prevent Saddam Hussein from starting other wars with his neighbors, and would eventually force him to disarm completely.

The U.S. policy toward Iraq changed in the wake of the September 11, 2001, terrorist attacks that destroyed the World Trade Center in New York City and damaged the Pentagon near Washington, D.C. The United States soon targeted the Taliban government of Afghanistan, which had supported and harbored al-Qaeda, the terrorist organization that had planned the September 11 attacks. A goal of the war in Afghanistan was to drive the Taliban from power. It became obvious that U.S. leaders wished to drive another Middle Eastern government from power as well—that of Saddam Hussein.

During his January 2002 State of the Union address, President George W. Bush—son of the president who, more than a decade earlier, had organized the coalition that won the Gulf War—called Iraq part of an "axis of evil." "Iraq continues to flaunt its hostility toward America and to support terror," the president noted. "The Iraqi regime has plotted to develop anthrax, and nerve gas, and nuclear weapons for over a decade. This is a regime that has already used poison gas to murder thousands of its own citizens—leaving the bodies of mothers huddled over their dead children. This is a regime that agreed to international inspections—then kicked out the inspectors. This is a regime that has something to hide from the civilized world."

Pressure from the United States led the United Nations to pass Resolution 1441 in November 2002. This resolution again demanded that Iraq destroy its chemical and biological weapons and provide unrestricted access for U.N. weapons inspectors. The resolution also said that Iraq would "face serious consequences" if it did not comply. The next month, U.N. inspectors returned to Iraq. Battling continued noncompliance from Iraqi leaders, the inspectors remained in the country until March 2003, when they were pulled out by the United Nations just before the start of the U.S.-led war to topple Saddam Hussein's regime.

To many people in the West, pictures of Saddam Hussein or television images from the two gulf wars are their only reference point for Iraq. Yet the region has a history that is long and glorious. Mesopotamia, the land between the Tigris and Euphrates Rivers in modern-day Iraq, is known as the "cradle of civilization" because the earliest known human civilization was established here more than 5,500 years ago. During the high point of the Arab Islamic civilization, from the 8th to the 13th centuries A.D., Baghdad was the seat of the Muslim **caliphs**, and thus the center of the Islamic world. Iraq was one of the first Arab nations to gain independence in the 20th century, and until the 1991 Gulf War it was considered an important Arab cultural center. The country is also important to the ***industrialized*** nations of the West because of its large supply of oil. Iraq's oil reserves are second only to Saudi Arabia's, and before the outbreak of the 2003 war the United States imported some 700,000 barrels of Iraqi oil each day.

It is a mistake to judge Iraq only in light of recent events. Long after the current wars and unrest in the country are forgotten, the illustrious history of this ancient land will be remembered.

This bridge across the Euphrates River was damaged during the 1991 Gulf War. The Euphrates, one of Iraq's two major rivers, originates in Turkey.

The Land

Iraq lies on the northern shore of the Arabian Gulf, more commonly known as the Persian Gulf among non-Arabs. Its small segment of coastline is situated between the much longer shorelines of Iran to its east and Kuwait to its south.

Iraq possesses a land area of some 168,754 square miles (437,072 square kilometers), making it slightly more than twice the size of Idaho. If Iraq were placed over the eastern part of the United States, its southern edge would rest at Raleigh, North Carolina, and its northern edge in Lake Ontario. The width of Iraq would stretch from Washington, D.C., in the east to Indianapolis, Indiana, in the west.

Iraq is surrounded by six countries, four of which are, like Iraq, populated by Arabs. Kuwait lies to the southeast of Iraq. To the south and southwest is the larger country of Saudi Arabia. Jordan, to the west of Iraq, shares a 113-mile (181-km) border. To the northwest is Syria, which borders

Iraq for 376 miles (605 km). The two non-Arab countries that border Iraq are Turkey, which lies to the north, and Iran, to the east.

THE RIVERS

Centuries before the name "Iraq" was used, the Greeks called the area between the Tigris and Euphrates Rivers "Mesopotamia," which means "between the rivers." It is along these rivers—especially at Baghdad and to the south—where most of Iraq's people have settled and where the country's heaviest industries have developed. From very early times, an irrigation system was developed that allowed agriculture to expand into the land between the two rivers. Thus the rivers have made the land fertile, helping people fortunate enough to live there to prosper.

The Tigris River has its source in the mountains of eastern Turkey. It enters Iraq in the far north and zigzags southeast through the country for 881 miles (1,418 km). After flowing through Baghdad, Iraq's capital city, the Tigris continues southeast to the town of Al Qurnah, where it meets the Euphrates River. The united rivers then become the Shatt al Arab, which flows south for about 100 miles (161 km) before entering the Persian Gulf. For much of this distance the river marks Iraq's southeastern border with Iran.

For centuries, the Tigris River flooded in late winter and early spring because of rains in the north. However, in the 1950s the Samarra Dam was built in central Iraq. When the river level is particularly high, the dam helps divert water into the Tharthar Reservoir, where it can be stored for later use.

Like the Tigris, the Euphrates River also originates in Turkey. It flows first through Syria and then enters Iraq in the northwest, running through the country for 743 miles (1,196 km). The Euphrates flows along a channel that is roughly parallel to that of the Tigris. As they flow through Iraq, the two rivers are between 25 and 100 miles (40 and 161 km) apart. Eventually, the Euphrates

Iraq's terrain consists mostly of low-lying plains and desert. The north and northeast are mountainous; marshes cover parts of the southeast, along the border with Iran.

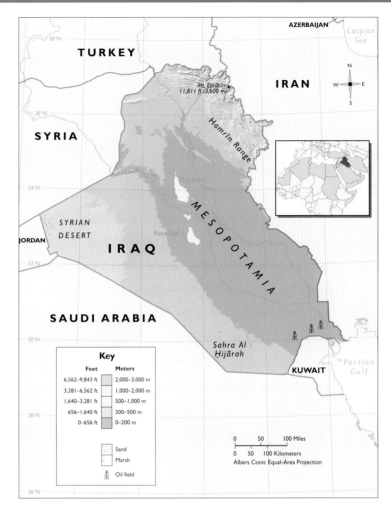

joins the Tigris at Al Qurnah.

Use of the water from the Euphrates River has led to disagreements between Turkey, Syria, and Iraq. All three countries are working on projects to use the river water to irrigate crops and generate hydroelectric power. Turkey has begun the Southeast Anatolia Project, which eventually will create 22 dams and 19 power plants where the Euphrates cascades down from the Anatolia Mountains. The Atatürk Dam in Turkey, one of the largest in the world, was completed in 1990 and has formed a reservoir of 315 square miles (815 sq km). In order to keep this reservoir full, Turkey creates regular interruptions in the flow of the Euphrates;

this affects the amount of water that flows into Syria and Iraq. Some estimates indicate that when the Southeast Anatolia Project is completed, it will reduce the flow from the Euphrates by about 40 percent to Syria and 90 percent to Iraq.

Syrian projects also reduce the amount of water from the Euphrates that reaches Iraq. The Al Thawrah Dam, built by Syria during the 1970s, created the Assad Reservoir. This significantly diminished the flow of water reaching Iraq.

If the level of the Euphrates River falls too low, water shortages in Iraq can result. Water from the Tharthar Reservoir, which is fed by the Tigris River, can be diverted into the Euphrates when it is low. In the past, however, the reservoir has not held an adequate supply to overcome the lack of water resulting from Syrian and Turkish projects. As a consequence, the relationship between the three nations has been strained at times. In 1998 Syria and Iraq agreed to work together to oppose the Southeast Anatolia Project, but their attempts to halt the project have been unsuccessful.

THE REGIONS

Geographically, the country of Iraq can be divided into four distinct regions. One is the southern **alluvial** plain, which begins just northwest of Baghdad and stretches southeast to the Persian Gulf. A second region is the desert plateau, which is located in western and southwestern Iraq on the borders of Syria, Jordan, and Saudi Arabia. The third region is the Jazirah (from the Arabic word for "island"). The Jazirah is a wedge-shaped territory in the northwest that touches Syria; it is bounded on the west by the Euphrates and on the east by the Tigris. A final region, the northeastern highlands, includes the Zagros Mountains, which are located along the border with Iran.

Vivian Block, who once taught English in the southern city of Basra, vividly remembers her impressions of the alluvial plain as she traveled by train north to Baghdad. "Looking out the window, we saw flat, arid ground. . . . The landscape, which was mostly desert, would have patches of green that a gardener attended to with daily irrigation. [I could see] alfalfa, onions, grasses, a celery-tasting herb called crufus, and parsley, as well as palm trees bearing dates."

The alluvial plain makes up about one-third of Iraq. The entire plain is flat with a low elevation, dropping from 80 feet above sea level near the city of Ramadi on the Euphrates to sea level in the south along the Persian Gulf.

The Geography of Iraq

Location: Middle East, bordering the Persian Gulf, between Iran and Kuwait

Area: (slightly more than twice the size of Idaho)
   total: 168,754 square miles (437,072 sq km)
   land: 166,858 square miles (432,162 sq km)
   water: 1,896 square miles (4,910 sq km)

Borders: Iran, 906 miles (1,458 km); Jordan, 113 miles (181 km); Kuwait, 149 miles (240 km); Saudi Arabia, 506 miles (814 km); Syria, 376 miles (605 km); Turkey, 219 miles (352 km)

Climate: mostly desert; mild to cool winters with dry, hot, cloudless summers; northern mountainous regions along Iranian and Turkish borders experience cold winters with occasionally heavy snows that melt in early spring, sometimes causing extensive flooding in central and southern Iraq

Terrain: mostly broad plains; reedy marshes along Iranian border in south with large flooded areas; mountains along borders with Iran and Turkey

Elevation extremes:
   lowest point: Persian Gulf, 0 feet
   highest point: Mt. Ebrahim, 11,811 feet (3,600 meters)

Natural hazards: dust storms, sandstorms, floods

Source: Adapted from CIA World Factbook, 2002.

Two large lakes dominate the landscape. One, Lake As-Saniyah, is just west of the Tigris and runs southwest from the town of Ali al-Gharbi for 75 miles (121 km). The second and more swampy lake, Al-Hammar, is farther south and extends from Basra to Suq ash-Shuyukh.

The Shatt al Arab is located in the south of the alluvial plain.

Located along the Iraq-Iran border, the Shatt al Arab has been a source of frequent conflict between the two countries.

Two of its tributaries are the Karkheh and the Karun Rivers, which flow into the Shatt from Iran just above Iraq's delta on the Persian Gulf. As a result of these rivers, the area near the Gulf is filled with small lakes and marshes that spread over the land-scape. The delta continues to grow as silt collects from the rivers. Continual dredging is necessary in order to keep the Shatt al Arab open for navigation to Basra.

A second distinct region is the desert plateau, located in western and southwestern Iraq. This barren area makes up about one-third of the country. It is the least-developed part of Iraq, and few people live in the desert, which is an extension of the Syrian and Arabian deserts. The flatness of the land is broken by a number of **wadis** running east and west, some for hundreds of miles. The few remaining Bedouins of Iraq live in this vast, dry area.

The western desert near Jordan rises to 100 feet (31 meters) and is called the Wadiyah. In the southern part of the desert plateau is a sandy, gravelly plain called Al-Diddibah, which borders the west-ern part of Kuwait. Its elevation ascends from about 300 feet (93 meters) near Kuwait to 3,000 feet (915 meters) where Saudi Arabia and Jordan intersect with Iraq to the west.

On the northern edge of the desert plateau is a highway that runs from Baghdad to Amman, the capital of Jordan, and to Damascus, the capital of Syria. Along this highway is the busy trad-ing center of Rutbah, one of the very few towns on the plateau.

The Jazirah region is located in the northwest, along the border with Syria. It is a desert plateau that descends from an average of 1,475 feet (450 meters) above sea level near Syria to about 260 feet (79 meters) above sea level just north of Baghdad. Most of the population of this region is located along the Tigris and Euphrates Rivers and in a small area of the north where rain allows agriculture. In the rest of the region the population is sparse and development is limited.

The rain-fed agricultural section of the Jazirah is near the Syrian border. There, wheat and barley can be grown without the necessity of irrigation. This area, which has been cultivated for thousands of years, was once known as the granary of the ancient world.

Mosul, Iraq's second-largest city, is the largest settlement within the Jazirah and the main center of activity for the northern third of the country. Mosul Province is the location of almost 80 percent

Mosul, situated along the western bank of the Tigris River, is northern Iraq's most important city. Seen here is one of the city's mosques.

of Iraq's vast oil reserves. At one time cotton was the main export of the province, and the word *muslin* (a type of cotton fabric) was derived from the city's name.

The fourth region of Iraq is called the northeastern highlands; it is part of a larger area known as Kurdistan, where most of Iraq's Kurdish population lives. The highlands contain rugged, almost inaccessible mountains. The elevation of this area ascends from 655 feet (200 meters) at the Tigris River to nearly 6,000 feet (1,830 meters) on the ridge tops. From there the mountain peaks soar to more than 11,000 feet (3,355 meters). The highest elevation in Iraq is Mount Ebrahim, which rises to a height of 11,811 feet (3,600 meters). At the higher elevations, the mountain peaks are covered with snow for half of the year. The Zagros Mountains are rugged, with only a few passes through them. The Rawanduze River Gorge, which connects Iraq and Iran, is the best known of these mountain passes.

The mountains contain Iraq's only forests. The steeper slopes permit only grazing for cattle, sheep, and goats, but on the lower, gentler slopes people cultivate fruit and nut trees.

Several streams in the highlands flow southeast into the Tigris, including the Khabur, Great Zab, Little Zab, Udhaym, and Diyala. The Iraqi government began hydraulic projects along some of these rivers in the 1950s. The Kukan Dam and reservoir and the Debs Dam were built on the Little Zab, and the Darbandikhan Dam and reservoir were constructed on the upper Diyala.

FLORA AND FAUNA

There is little vegetation in most of Iraq. In the Zagros Mountains, forests of oak, maple, and hawthorn trees still exist, although in recent years the size of these forests has been reduced because of overcutting. The rest of the country contains few trees, except for the date palm and the poplar, which grow along the rivers.

Although millennia of human habitation have reduced the amount of wildlife living in Iraq, many animals still make this land their home. Mammals that can be seen in Iraq include cheetahs, gazelles, antelopes, wild asses, hyenas, wolves, jackals, wild pigs, and rabbits. Many birds of prey, such as vultures, buzzards, ravens, and hawks, continue to soar above the landscape. Other birds common to Iraq include ducks, geese, and partridges. Closer to the ground, numerous types of reptiles and lizards can be found. There are many domesticated animals, such as camels, oxen, water buffalo, and horses, and flocks of sheep and goats can be found on mountainsides.

THE CLIMATE AND THE WINDS

The climate of Iraq is fairly similar throughout the country, with the exception of the north. Mosul's January temperature averages 44° Fahrenheit (6° Celsius); in July, the average temperature in Mosul is about 90°F (32°C). Winter and summer temperatures are much lower in the high elevations of the Zagros Mountains. Baghdad's average temperature is about 50°F (10°C) in January and about 95°F (35°C) in July. Temperatures in the southern alluvial plain, however, can reach 123°F (51°C) in the summer.

There are two wind patterns in the country. The eastern wind, called *sharki*, is hot, dry, and dusty; it can gust at up to 50 miles per hour (81 km per hour) and create massive dust storms. The *sharki* winds can occur throughout the year, although they are more frequent during the summer months. The other wind is known as *shammal*; it is a steady, gentle wind that comes from the north and brings great relief during the extreme heat of the summer months.

The northeastern highlands receive ample rainfall from October to May, so the lower levels of this region are suitable for farming and are home to a large population. By contrast, the southeastern alluvial plain receives only about 6 inches (15 centimeters) of rain each year. As a result, agriculture there depends entirely upon irrigation. There is almost no rainfall at all in the western and southwestern desert plateau, which covers about one-third of Iraq.

Mesopotamia produced the world's earliest known civilization, Sumer, as well as the oldest known system of writing, cuneiform. The clay tablet shown here, which is covered with cuneiform writing, is important for another reason: it is the prologue to the Code of Hammurabi, one of the earliest legal codes, which dates to the 18th century B.C.

History

In 1901 a group of French archaeologists traveled to Mesopotamia to search for the remains of an ancient civilization. As the archaeologists dug into the sun-baked earth, they hit a large object. Digging carefully, they uncovered an eight-foot-long block of black basalt. Across the face of the huge stone were words carved in a language unfamiliar to the archaeologists. It was evidence of the powerful kingdom they had sought.

When the writings on the basalt slab were translated, they were found to be the laws of Hammurabi, a great ruler of Babylon who had lived around 1750 B.C. The Code of Hammurabi, as the laws are called, is one of the earliest written legal systems; it gives modern students valuable insight into the structure of ancient Mesopotamian society.

By the time of Hammurabi, civilization in Mesopotamia had already existed for some two and a half millennia.

Mesopotamia is often called the "cradle of civilization" because archaeologists believe that it is the place where human settlements first evolved into a society with complex social and political organization and advanced cultural achievements. **Nomadic** hunter-gatherers may have settled in the area between the Tigris and Euphrates Rivers as early as 9000 B.C. They used the river water for agriculture and began to domesticate animals such as sheep and dogs. As these hunters tied themselves to the land and depended on farming for their food, they began to build villages. Over thousands of years, these would evolve into city-states and, eventually, kingdoms and empires.

Sumer, considered the world's first civilization, was the most famous of the early Mesopotamian empires. By the 24th century B.C., the Sumerian cities had been unified into an empire. The Sumerians are credited with many inventions. One of these was cuneiform writing, in which long reeds were used to make wedge-shaped characters on tablets of soft clay; these tablets were later baked to make them hard, preserving the writing. Hundreds of thousands of cuneiform tablets have been found and translated, giving insights into daily life in Mesopotamia. Sumerians also developed such important tools as the wheel and the plow, and they created a form of banking.

As the centuries passed, empires rose and fell in Mesopotamia. One of the greatest of the later ones was Assyria, the largest empire the ancient world had ever seen. The empire lasted from about 1400 B.C. to 612 B.C. At the height of their influence the Assyrians controlled land from the Mediterranean Sea to the Caspian Sea, and from the Persian Gulf to the Red Sea. The ruins of Nineveh, the capital of Assyria, are located near the city of Mosul, Iraq.

In 612 B.C. Nineveh was destroyed by another growing Mesopotamian power, the Babylonians. One of the most influential Babylonian rulers was King Nebuchadnezzar, who built Babylon into the most beautiful city in the ancient world. He created the famous "hanging gardens," with trees, plants, and flowers growing on a tiered structure held by arches 400 feet (122 meters) above the ground. The Hanging Gardens of Babylon were proclaimed one of the Seven Wonders of the Ancient World.

However, Nebuchadnezzar's descendants did not remain in power for long. Babylon fell to the Medes and Persians (people from the modern-day state of Iran) in 539 B.C. Under Cyrus the Great, the Persian Achaemenid Empire was established; the Achaemenids ruled Mesopotamia and most of the Middle East for the next 250 years. During this time the communities of Mesopotamia fell into decline, and Babylon and other cities withered and decayed.

In the fourth century B.C., the Achaemenids were defeated by the armies of the Macedonian conqueror Alexander the Great. Alexander's conquests brought Hellenistic culture to the region, and he planned to rebuild Babylon and make it an administrative center of his vast empire. However, Alexander died in Babylon in 323 B.C., before these plans could be carried out. Alexander's Greek generals

The remains of Nebuchadnezzar's palace in Babylon. Nebuchadnezzar, a seventh-century B.C. king of Babylon, built the Hanging Gardens of Babylon, one of the Seven Wonders of the Ancient World.

remained in power in Mesopotamia until 126 B.C., when the Parthians, a people from northern Persia, took control of the region.

The Parthian rulers who controlled Mesopotamia were often in conflict with the Roman Empire, which controlled the lands adjacent to the Mediterranean Sea (such as Syria). Roman legions occupied Mesopotamia for brief periods—from A.D. 98 to 117 and from 193 to 211. After 227, a new group came to power in Persia: the Sassanids. They soon took control of Mesopotamia as well.

After the Roman Empire split during the fourth century, the Sassanids continued fighting with the Eastern Roman, or Byzantine, Empire. From the city of Constantinople, in modern-day Turkey, the Christian Byzantines dominated the eastern Mediterranean and North Africa. The Sassanids and the Byzantines struggled with one another for centuries, competing for territories and trade routes. But by the seventh century, the world of the Middle East underwent a radical change with the rise of a new religion, Islam.

THE RISE OF ISLAM

Around 570, Muhammad ibn Abdullah was born on the Arabian Peninsula. For many years the communities of Arabia had been prosperous because of trade. Muhammad lived in the city of Mecca; when he grew up he married a wealthy widow and became a successful merchant.

At the time, the people of the Arabian Peninsula were pagans who worshipped many gods. One god, Allah, was believed to have created the earth, but in general Allah was given no more or less attention than any of the other Arab gods. According to tradition, however, Muhammad grew up worshipping only Allah.

When he was about 40 years old, Muhammad received a series of divine messages, which said that Allah was the only true God. Muhammad was told to spread this message to the people of Arabia. He began to call on his neighbors in Mecca to give up their other, false gods and surrender their lives to Allah. (The word *Islam* comes from an Arabic word meaning "submission" or "surrender.")

At first, the people of Mecca tolerated the teachings of Muhammad, though he attracted few followers. Eventually, however, Mecca's pagan leaders decided to do away with the annoying preacher. They plotted to kill Muhammad, but he got wind of the plot. In 622 Muhammad and his followers fled Mecca, journeying to another city, Medina, which was several hundred miles to the north.

The people of Medina welcomed Muhammad and listened to his message. The ranks of Muslims—as followers of Islam are called—grew rapidly.

Two years after the flight to Medina, Muhammad's followers and

Around A.D. 610 Muhammad, an Arab living in Mecca, was visited in a cave by the Angel Gabriel, who commanded him to proclaim the word of Allah (God). Islam's beginnings can be traced to that event, which is depicted in this colored engraving.

a force of Meccans fought a major battle at the village of Badr. The Muslims won decisively, but in the ensuing years the two sides fought many skirmishes and an occasional pitched battle. Finally, in 629, Muhammad returned to Mecca with a small army. The people of Mecca surrendered without bloodshed, and many converted to Islam.

Muhammad's disciples wrote down and organized his teachings into a book, the Qur'an (or Koran). Devout Muslims consider the Qur'an to be the direct word of God, and therefore a holy, perfect scripture.

After the capitulation of Mecca, Muhammad sent envoys throughout the Arab world, inviting the scattered tribes to become Muslims. Most of the tribes quickly joined; those that did not were conquered by the growing Muslim armies and forced to convert at the point of a sword. By the time of Muhammad's death in 632, Islam had spread throughout the Arabian Peninsula and north into Syria.

Islam came to the region of modern-day Iraq shortly after Muhammad's death. In 634 the Islamic caliph, who was selected to lead the Muslims after Muhammad, sent his armies on raids into Mesopotamia. In a series of battles between 634 and 636, the Arabs soundly defeated the Sassanid forces, despite being outnumbered six to one.

At this time, most people living in Mesopotamia followed Christianity. The Muslims allowed them to practice their religion, so long as they paid a special tax to the conquering Arabs. Arab settlers also poured into Mesopotamia from Arabia, living along the fertile plains of the Tigris and Euphrates. Over time, the natives of Mesopotamia intermarried with the Arab newcomers, and most converted to Islam.

The Iraq area was the site of a major division in the Islamic faith—the break between Sunni and Shiite Muslims. The split arose out of a disagreement over who should be the caliph. Most Muslims supported the selection of the caliph based on his piety; these became known as the Sunni Muslims. However, a minority insisted that the caliph should be a member of Muhammad's family—particularly, the prophet's son-in-law Ali and his descendants. These Muslims became known as Shiites. The Shiites also felt that the Sunni caliphs misinterpreted the Qur'an. The two groups fought for power until the Battle of Karbala in 680, when the Shiite leader Hussein was slain along with his family and 200 of his followers. Iraqi cities such as An Najaf and Karbala remain important shrines for Shiite Muslims today. After the defeat of the Shiites, the Sunni caliphs maintained their control over Islam.

For the next seven centuries, two Sunni dynasties ruled the Muslims—the Umayyads from 661 to 750 and the Abbasids from 750 to 1258. The caliphs ruled the spreading Islamic empire first from Medina, and then from Damascus, Syria. In 762 the administrative center was moved to a new city on the Tigris River, called Madinat as-Salam ("the City of Peace"), although many people still knew it by the name of a small town that had been on that site before—Baghdad.

During the eighth century, Muslim culture blossomed in Baghdad. Literature, science, art, and mathematics flourished, and Baghdad became one of the world's leading cities. The caliphs encouraged the growth of knowledge by opening schools that attracted scholars from all over. The writings of ancient Greece and Rome were translated into Arabic and preserved in libraries and universities in Baghdad and other cities. Many of these important writings had been lost in the West when barbarians destroyed the Roman Empire; they would be rediscovered by European scholars centuries later. The 8th through the 12th centuries are often considered to be the golden age of the Arab Islamic civilization.

The area of modern-day Iraq continued to be at the center of the Islamic civilization until the 13th century. During the early years of that century, the Mongols had spread their control east from Asia into Persia under the great leader Genghis Khan. In 1258 Mongol armies sacked Baghdad. The city was destroyed, and most of the inhabitants were slaughtered—in fact, the Mongol leader Hülegü Khan, grandson of Genghis Khan, made a pyramid from the skulls of poets, scholars, and religious leaders in Baghdad. During the next few centuries, control of Mesopotamia alternated between the Mongols and local rulers; in general, however, the region fell into decline.

CONFLICT OVER THE REGION

By the 15th century, a new power was rising in the Middle East—the Ottoman Turks. In 1453 the Ottomans conquered Constantinople, ending the 1,000-year history of the Byzantine Empire. The Ottoman Turks were Sunni Muslims who were dedicated to the faith, but they also wanted to expand their own power throughout the region. By the early 16th century, the Ottomans were entending their empire into Syria, Egypt, and Arabia, and they turned their sights on Mesopotamia to the south.

During the same period, the Safavid Empire had come to power in Persia to the east. The Safavid rulers declared Shia Islam to be the official religion of Persia, and they wanted to control Iraq in part because it contained the important Shiite shrines at An Najaf and Karbala. Fighting between the Ottomans and Safavids continued for more than a century. The Safavid armies conquered Mesopotamia in 1509, but the Ottomans took control of the region in 1535. The Safavids retook Baghdad in 1623, but lost the city to the Ottomans in 1638.

The Ottoman Empire would maintain control over Mesopotamia until the early years of the 20th century. An Ottoman governor was placed in Baghdad, and important families were given positions in the Ottoman government. The Ottomans divided Mesopotamia into

The Mongols' sack of Baghdad in 1258 was considerably more violent than this illustration from a Persian manuscript might indicate. The conquerors laid waste to the magnificent city and slaughtered most of its inhabitants. The Mongol leader, Hülegü Khan, even constructed a pyramid from the skulls of the dead.

three provinces—a northern province governed from Mosul, a central province ruled from Baghdad, and a southern province controlled from Basra. Outside of these cities, however, the power of the Ottoman officials was limited. Instead, local tribal chiefs called **sheikhs** had the real authority in rural Mesopotamia. Although they paid taxes to the Ottomans, these sheikhs had a great deal of independence.

By the end of the 19th century, widespread unrest had developed in Mesopotamia. This occurred in part because of a land law that had been passed by the Ottoman government in 1858. Before

The Ottoman Turks capture Constantinople, 1453. During the following century, the Ottoman Empire extended its control into Kurdistan and Mesopotamia, in present-day Iraq. Ottoman influence in the region would last until the second decade of the 20th century.

passage of this law, the Arabs did not recognize private ownership of land. Those who used the land and could hold it occupied the land. But under the land law, the Ottoman government allowed people to register their claim to land, and the government would recognize them as the owners of the property.

The land law affected the way power was distributed in the region. Traditionally, Arab sheikhs had ruled with the consent of others in the tribe, and they were supposed to make decisions based on what was best for the tribe. But after the rural sheikhs and the important families in Baghdad registered their claims to land, they were obliged to support the Ottoman government, which could back up their land claims with military force. Most of the ordinary tribesmen became little more than tenant farmers, with their labor enriching the landowning families.

During the 19th century, contact with the nations of Europe began to increase. The opening of the Suez Canal by France in 1869, and the strong presence of Great Britain, which had treaties with a number of small Arab kingdoms on the Gulf, brought the people of Mesopotamia into contact with Western ideas and technology.

Meanwhile, at the very heart of the Ottoman Empire in Istanbul, a new ideology—***nationalism***—was beginning to supplant the old religion-based legitimacy of the empire. Nationalist Turks wished to create a ***secular*** Turkish state, in which all of the people would share a common ethnic background, culture, or heritage. In 1908 a group of young Turkish officers (who became known in the West as the "Young Turks") mounted a resistance movement against Sultan Abdul Hamid II. Taking control of parliament, they staged an election for a new parliament representative of Turkey. Rule by the Young Turks was followed by the Committee of Union and Progress (CUP), which controlled the remnants of the Ottoman Empire until 1918. This period of Turkish nationalism resulted in political and cultural repression of Arabs in the Ottoman Empire. Use of the Arabic language was banned, and leaders who supported the idea of Arab nationalism were arrested.

Everything would change after the start of the First World War in 1914. The Ottoman Empire entered the war on the side of the Central Powers, Germany and Austria-Hungary. Great Britain, fighting on the side of the Allies, landed troops near Basra in November 1914 to seize this Ottoman territory on the Gulf. By March 1917, British troops had captured Baghdad; by the time the war ended, the British controlled the region as far north as Mosul. Great Britain also encouraged the Arabs to rise up against their Ottoman rulers. Under the leadership of Hussein bin Ali, the sharif of Mecca, some Arabs launched a revolt in 1916. At the war's conclusion in 1918, Arab forces controlled much of present-day Jordan, Syria, and the Arabian Peninsula.

THE BRITISH MANDATE

After the end of the First World War, an armistice line was drawn north of Mosul, leaving the British firmly in control of all three of the former Ottoman provinces in Mesopotamia.

The British and their allies had encouraged the Great Arab Revolt by making vague promises to Arab nationalists that the region would be united as an Arab state. However, when the war ended, a newly created international organization, the League of Nations, divided the Arab region into a number of smaller territories. At the 1919 Paris Peace Conference, Great Britain was given a **mandate** to rule Mesopotamia, as well as other territories in the Middle East. The area of the British Mesopotamian mandate was also given a new name, Iraq, from an Arabic word meaning "shoreline." This term had previously been used to designate the southern part of the country.

Some of the Arab leaders felt the British mandate was just a way to bring their country into the British Empire. They had a legitimate reason to worry, because British officials were discussing whether England should directly rule the territory or help it develop self-government. Under the League of Nations' mandate system, the established European governments were supposed to help the former Ottoman territories build governments and rule themselves. But the European powers seemed to be interested in making the mandate areas part of their colonial empires. France, for example, had been given the League of Nations mandate to rule Syria and

Lebanon in April 1920. The month before, a Syrian national congress had selected a king for Syria—Faisal, the son of Sharif Hussein bin Ali. After the French arrived, they forced Faisal to flee the country, then set up their own government.

There were other problems with the mandate that created Iraq. For one, the population of the region was quite disparate. For example, more than 50 percent of the people of Iraq were Arab Shiite Muslims, about 20 percent were Arab Sunni Muslims, and about 20 percent were Kurdish Sunni Muslims. There were also Kurdish

The decisions of the so-called Big Four leaders (from left: Prime Minister David Lloyd George of Great Britain, Prime Minister Vittorio Orlando of Italy, Prime Minister Georges Clemenceau of France, and President Woodrow Wilson of the United States) during the Paris Peace Conference of 1919 shaped the world—often in unforeseen ways—for decades to come. It was at Paris that the nation of Iraq was created.

Shiites and Arab Christians living in the country. In addition to the historic differences between the Sunni and Shiite Muslims, there are important ethnic and cultural differences between Arabs and Kurds, who have their own language and traditions. However, under the centuries of Ottoman rule, the minority Sunni Arabs had gained a great amount of land and power; the Shiites had been subject to Ottoman discrimination. Most of the government officials in Baghdad and officers in the army were Arab Sunni Muslims, and they were determined to maintain their control over the region by resisting the British.

By mid-1920, central Iraq was in the hands of the Sunni Arabs; however, by the end of October 1920 the British had brought the revolt under control. But when Britain created a new government for Iraq, most of the government officials and the officers of the new Iraqi army were members of the Sunni Arab families that had held power under the Ottoman Turks. The British, though, chose the

Though he had never even visited Iraq, Faisal I, a member of the Hashemite family, was the British choice as Iraq's king.

king of Iraq—36-year-old Prince Faisal, who assumed the throne on August 23, 1921.

King Faisal did not have much support from the leading families and tribes of Iraq, who saw the king as a foreigner (he was a member of the Hashemite family of the western Arabian Peninsula) and a puppet of the Western powers. Faisal's goal was to develop Iraq into a unified country with loyalty to a central government, but the many diverse groups in Iraq and the political power of the Sunni Muslim minority would limit success.

The Kurdish people of northern Iraq also opposed the monarchy. The 1920 treaty that established Iraq and other countries initially called for a Kurdish state in the mountainous region known as Kurdistan, which included parts of Iraq, Turkey, Iran, Armenia, and Syria. However, the new governments of these areas decided against establishing a Kurdish state. In Iraq, it was determined that the Kurds should have some control over the government of their northern province. For the Kurds, however, this was not enough: they revolted against the British-supported monarchy from 1922 to 1924 and again in 1932. Both times their attempts to separate were crushed.

As the capital of the monarchy, Baghdad became the center of power. Land became the reward for those who found favor with the king. Iraqis who gained influential government positions used their authority to reward family members or friends. And the monarchy remained subordinate to Great Britain, which exercised extensive control over Iraq's internal affairs as well as its foreign relations.

OIL AND THE MONARCHY

During the 1920s, oil became an important element in the development of Iraq. Before World War I, the Ottoman Turks had agreed to allow the Turkish Petroleum Company—a group of British, Dutch, French, and American investors—to search for oil in

Mesopotamia. After the Iraqi monarchy was formed, the Western powers pressured King Faisal to give up Iraq's right to the country's oil in exchange for annual royalty payments.

In 1927 oil was discovered in northeast Iraq near Kirkuk. The Iraqi government agreed to give the oil company (renamed the Iraq Petroleum Company) exclusive rights to explore for oil in all of northeastern Iraq. By 1931 oil revenues made up 20 percent of government income, and oil had begun to be a source of power to those in office.

During this time, however, Arab nationalists continued to oppose both the British presence in Iraq and the monarchy of King Faisal. In 1929 Great Britain announced its plan to end its mandate over Iraq and allow the country to become independent. In October 1932 Iraq joined the League of Nations as an independent nation. However, British influence over the king remained strong, and a treaty between Britain and Iraq permitted British forces to use air bases in the country.

Continuing tensions between Arabs and Kurds, as well as among Sunnis, Shiites, and Christians, prevented the government from achieving stability. There were also problems with the region's borders, which had been drawn arbitrarily by the European powers. The boundaries limited trade outside of the country, contributing to an economic depression, and also led to skirmishes between Iraq and its neighbors Saudi Arabia, Iran, Turkey, and Syria.

When King Faisal died suddenly in 1933, the crown went to his 21-year-old son, Ghazi. However, the new king was unable to manage the factions within Iraq's government. During the years of his rule, many problems surfaced or got worse. Tribes in the remote areas of Iraq revolted against the central government, and in the north the Kurds tried to gain independence. At the same time, Iran reopened an old dispute with Iraq over the use of the Shatt al Arab waterway, part of the border between their two countries. To gain more control of the waterway, Iran challenged the border.

At the height of the tensions, in 1939, King Ghazi was killed in a car crash. His son, Faisal II, became king, but because the boy was only three years old, his uncle, Abdulillah, became **regent**, with authority to rule until Faisal II was old enough to take the throne.

In September 1939 the Second World War began in Europe when the armies of Nazi Germany invaded Poland. As the German war machine rolled over Europe, crushing France by June 1940, Great Britain found itself in a desperate struggle against the Nazis. Because many Arab nationalists in Iraq did not like British influence over their government, some officers in the Iraqi army supported the German dictator Adolf Hitler. In 1941 these officers revolted against the administration of Abdulillah, forcing the regent to flee the country.

To restore order, British troops landed in Iraq, put down the **coup**, and placed Abdulillah back in charge of the government. When he was returned to power, Abdulillah tried to purge Iraq of those who dissented with his rule, imprisoning or executing many nationalists and establishing tight restrictions.

After World War II ended in 1945, Iraqi society grew more open. The press, which had been censored during the war, was allowed greater freedom. Political parties, once banned, were given permission to organize. When the economy weakened, though, unrest grew. The government again began to limit freedom, increasing dissatisfaction with the monarchy. Other events in the Middle East would also lead to unrest, particularly the conflict in the area of British Palestine.

After the First World War, the region along the eastern Mediterranean coast known as Palestine had been placed under British rule by the League of Nations. In ancient times the region had been the homeland of the Jewish people; some Jews had never left the land, while others arrived as settlers during the 19th and early 20th centuries. At the same time, Arabs who had lived in the land for centuries were not happy about the arrival of these Jewish settlers, and they often attacked settlements. During World War II, the Nazis had attempted to carry out Hitler's "final solution"—the extermination of the Jews—and approximately 6 million European Jews were killed in concentration camps. After the end of the war, many survivors of the Holocaust left Europe for Palestine, where they hoped to build a Jewish state. Violence between Jews and Arabs began to escalate.

In 1947 the United Nations, an international organization that replaced the failed League of Nations, proposed dividing Palestine into Arab and Jewish states, with Jerusalem, a city regarded as holy by Jews, Muslims, and Christians, to be open to everyone under the auspices of the U.N. Great Britain, which still ruled the area under its League of Nations mandate, did not agree with this decision and announced its intention to withdraw from Palestine in May 1948. The Palestinian Arabs also voiced their opposition to the U.N. partition plan, and with other Arab countries they made plans to destroy the Jewish settlers once the British pulled out.

Israel declared its independence on May 15, 1948, the day after the British left Palestine. The United States and the U.S.S.R. quickly recognized Israel as an independent state. But Arab armies from Egypt, Jordan, Syria, and Iraq immediately attacked Israel. Iraq provided the largest force—some 15,000 well-trained soldiers. The Arabs expected a quick victory. However, to their surprise—and to the surprise of the world—the determined Israelis outfought the Arabs and expanded their territory before a cease-fire ended the conflict in early 1949.

The new Jewish state soon had a large influx of immigrants. Jewish communities had existed in Arab lands for hundreds of years, but many Jews—aware now of a growing hostility toward them in the Arab world—chose to move to Israel. In 1947 an estimated 117,000

Jews had lived in Iraq; many of their ancestors had been brought to Babylon as captives after the conquest of Jerusalem around 597 B.C. By 1952 Jews living in Iraq numbered fewer than 5,000.

The 1950s also saw oil become an even more important part of Iraq's economy. By 1952 most of the money brought into Iraq came from the production of oil. As a result, huge amounts of money were now available to those who controlled the government.

During the 1940s and 1950s, Nuri al-Said was an important political figure in Iraq. His views favored the countries of the West—in particular, Great Britain and the United States. He held the office of prime minister several times—but even when he was not in public office, Said wielded great power in the country. With his pro-Western position, he angered many Iraqis who still resented the British presence in Iraq's affairs. Said was not interested in democracy, however, and built his own power on personal relationships and ties with important families within Iraq. He formed a political party, Hizb al-Ittihad Al Dusturi (the Constitutional Union Party), and used it for his own advancement.

After the Constitutional Union Party won a majority in the 1953 elections, Nuri became Iraq's minister of defense. One of his goals was to make the army completely obedient to the state, because he realized that an independent army corps could be dangerous to his ambitions. Although most of the senior officers supported Nuri, many younger officers did not. They secretly formed a group called the Free Officers and began to talk about resistance to the government.

The concept of Arab nationalism—of building a single state in which the Arabs were united—had never gone away. The problem with this concept was that nearly every Arab leader thought he should be the head of the united Arab state. But during this time the strongest of the Arab leaders was Gamal Abdel Nasser, who had come to power in Egypt in 1952. Nasser wanted to bring about a pan-Arab state, headed by Egypt, the largest Arab country. He also wanted to modernize Egypt and undertook a series of development projects. In 1956, after British and U.S. financial assistance dried up following Egypt's purchase of Soviet arms, Nasser announced that he would nationalize the Suez Canal. This decision sparked a joint attack, for the purposes of securing the canal, by France, Britain, and Israel. But the actions of these American allies—at the height of the Cold War—worried U.S. leaders, who feared that permitting the seizure of the canal would drive the Arab states to the side of the communist U.S.S.R. The United States used its influence to force the British, French, and Israelis to withdraw.

Though the Egyptian army had been defeated on the battlefield, Nasser became a hero in the Arab world. His defiance of the West inspired the Arab nationalists. In Iraq, the Free Officers admired Nasser and wanted their own country to follow the same independent, anti-Western course. Demonstrations against the monarchy were held in the major cities of Iraq throughout 1956.

YEARS OF REVOLUTION AND UNREST

More Iraqi military officers joined the Free Officers after the 1956 Suez crisis. By 1958 the Free Officers had agreed that they would overthrow the monarchy. They secretly formed a Supreme Committee, with one of their officers, General Abd al-Karim Qasim, as chairman.

Although King Faisal II had come of age in May 1953, the regent Abdulillah continued to exercise great influence in the government, as did Nuri al-Said.

In 1958 two of the largest Arab states, Egypt and Syria, announced they would form a political organization, the United Arab Republic. This merger would increase their influence over their neighbors. In response, the Hashemite rulers of Jordan and Iraq formed their own organization, the Arab Union, in February 1958.

When unrest developed in Lebanon during July 1958, Nuri al-Said decided to send Iraqi troops into Jordan to support the pro-West Hashemite government there. On July 13, Iraqi troops stationed in eastern Iraq were ordered to Jordan. On the way, as the army passed through Baghdad, General Abd al-Karim Qasim ordered the soldiers to seize all important buildings in Baghdad, including the radio station. When they controlled the radio and government buildings, the Free Officers announced that they had overthrown the monarchy and were forming a republic. Nuri al-Said, King Faisal II, Abdulillah, and other government leaders and members of the royal family were taken from their homes and executed.

Qasim became prime minister, minister of defense, and commander-in-chief of the military, while another officer, Colonel Abd al-Salam Arif, took over other important leadership positions. It wasn't long, however, before the two disagreed on the direction the

Prince Abdulillah, the Iraqi regent, hands over power to Faisal II in a ceremony on the latter's 18th birthday, May 2, 1953. Despite the end of his official role, Abdulillah continued to exert considerable influence on the new Iraqi king.

new government should take. Arif wanted the Arab people to be united in a single country, and he was willing to join with Egypt's Nasser to make that happen. Qasim, on the other hand, wanted to see Iraq become a strong Arab power, and he did not want to be subordinate to Nasser.

Qasim repressed all opposition, and soon he imprisoned Arif and other Free Officers who disagreed with him. He maintained control in the same way that Iraqi leaders had under the monarchy—rewarding those who supported him and dealing harshly with those who did not. Street demonstrations became common as different groups struggled for power, both within the civilian government and the military.

Political parties began to develop increased influence in Iraqi politics. Since the Iraqi Communist Party was the only long-established political party in Iraq, Qasim looked to it for support. It was composed mostly of the thwarted and powerless, the Shia and Kurds. Another group, the Baath (Renaissance) Party, had been active in Iraq for several years; the Baath Party was a small, secretive group of Arab nationalists. The original Baath Party had formed in Syria in the 1940s, and a branch of the party had emerged in Iraq during 1951. The party appealed to some young people in Iraq because Baath leaders criticized the power of the landowners and emphasized the need for pan-Arabism.

The Arab nationalists created an uprising against the Communists in Mosul in March 1959. Qasim stamped out the revolt with a sweeping massacre. Another demonstration occurred in the city of Kirkuk on July 14, 1959, the anniversary of the overthrow of the monarchy. Qasim again ruthlessly suppressed the dissenters and arrested many Arab nationalists leaders.

As Qasim grew more and more unpopular in Mosul and Kirkuk, the leaders of the Baath Party decided they could attract new followers by assassinating him. Their attempt in October of 1959 was unsuccessful, although the Baath conspirators killed a guard and wounded Qasim. One of the assassins was a 22-year-old named Saddam Hussein, who escaped arrest by fleeing to Cairo, Egypt.

In June 1961, the nearby country of Kuwait declared its independence after years of British rule. Qasim publicly claimed that Kuwait rightfully belonged to Iraq and that he wanted it to be annexed to his country. He argued that the League of Nations should have included that territory in the nation of Iraq in 1923, since it had been part of the Basra province under the Ottoman Empire. Qasim further argued that the British had deliberately separated it from Iraq to block Iraq's access to the Persian Gulf.

The British, fearing that Qasim would seize Iraq's defenseless neighbor, sent troops to Kuwait. The Arab League, to show its opposition to Qasim's claims, admitted Kuwait as a member. By the end

A July 1958 coup toppled the Iraqi monarchy and brought Colonel Abd al-Salam Arif (left) and General Abd al-Karim Qasim (right) to power. The two soon had a falling-out, however, and Qasim ordered his rival arrested.

of the summer, troops from the Arab League replaced the British soldiers. As a result, Iraq broke off diplomatic relations with many Arab countries. This unsuccessful attempt by Qasim to acquire Kuwait further weakened his reputation within the Iraqi army and his authority as leader of Iraq.

In spite of his disfavor within the army, Qasim became popular with the Iraqi people because of his many reforms that helped the lower classes. He improved education and health care and began a land reform program that gave poor people farms of 20 to 40 acres.

However, Qasim allowed no representative government and became more and more dictatorial. His harsh policies caused many political groups to meet secretly. By the early 1960s, the Baathists had infiltrated the Qasim government and were able to enlist many civilians and army officers into their party.

But it was the continued dissatisfaction of Iraq's Kurdish population that ultimately undermined Qasim's dictatorship. The Kurds had supported the 1958 overthrow of the monarchy; in exchange Qasim had promised the Kurds a measure of equality with the Arab Iraqis. This never materialized, and by September 1961 the Kurds rose up against the Qasim government. Qasim ordered the bombing of Kurdish villages.

The Kurds asked the Baath Party for help, promising to stop fighting if Qasim were removed from power. On February 8, 1963, military units loyal to the Baath Party assassinated an army officer who supported Qasim. After a day of fighting between the Baathist units and troops loyal to the government, Qasim was captured, brought before a military tribunal, and sentenced to death. Abd al-Salam Arif, who had been imprisoned by Qasim, was freed and named president.

After the overthrow of Qasim, no plan had been developed to put a new government into place. The first action of the Baath Party's leaders was to eliminate Qasim's supporters and try to solidify their own position. Almost 3,000 were killed in the fighting that followed. The National Guard of the Baath Party, a military force that had grown to 30,000 men, carried out attacks against those the party's leaders felt were not in complete agreement with Baathist beliefs. The Guard arrested and tortured many innocent people. The Baath Party seemed especially determined to take the Kurdish territory and its wealth of oil. They bombed some Kurdish villages and demolished others with tanks, killing hundreds of Kurds.

This repression turned many Iraqis against the Baath Party. On November 18, 1963, President Arif ordered the military to attack the Baath National Guard in Baghdad, in order to solidify his own control over the country. To protect his government against further coups, Arif formed the Republican Guard from members of his own clan, stationing them around the city of Baghdad. Then he purged the government of its Baathist members.

Less than three years later, in April 1966, President Arif died in a helicopter crash, and his brother, General Abd al-Rahman Arif, became president. The new leader arranged a cease-fire with the Kurds. He also permitted the people of Iraq more freedom than they had enjoyed under any government since the overthrow of the monarchy. However, in 1966 the Baath Party was renewed under the leadership of General Ahmed Hassan al-Bakr, who appointed his cousin Saddam Hussein deputy secretary-general of the Regional Command of the Baath Party.

In 1968 three key officers in the Iraqi army led a coup that over-threw Arif's government and sent Arif into exile. Hassan al-Bakr became the president of Iraq, and Abd al-Razzaq al-Nayif, one of the three coup leaders, became prime minister.

The Baath Party learned from its mistakes of 1963. When the party seized power in 1968, it again did so with the help of military officers. However, soon after the coup the Baath leaders moved against the military. Al-Nayif was exiled, top officers were purged,

Abd al-Rahman Arif, who assumed the presidency in 1966, relaxed government restrictions on personal freedom and arranged a cease-fire with the Kurds. But within two years his regime was overthrown by the socialist Baath Party.

and key Baath Party members were installed in the leadership positions. To inspire fear in anyone who might oppose his rule, Hassan al-Bakr ordered some of his opponents hanged in the streets of Baghdad. Saddam Hussein was placed in charge of the Baath Party's militia, and he showed no mercy when dealing with dissidents.

In 1972 Iraq nationalized its oil fields—meaning that revenue from Iraqi petroleum production would no longer be split with foreign companies managing the oil fields. The foreign companies had received half of the profits. As a result, a torrent of money flowed to al-Bakr's government. By 1975 Iraq was earning some $8 billion a year from the sale of oil.

This wealth enabled the Baathist government not only to build up the military, but also to pour money into health care and education. Baghdad went through a building boom and turned from a dusty town of mud-brick houses into a modern city of high-rises.

But al-Bakr faced several problems as he and his associates tried to reinforce their hold on the government. Iran had often fought with Iraq over their common border on the Shatt al Arab, and in the early 1970s Iran was once again insisting that the border between the two countries should lie in the center of the waterway. This change would give Iran more control over the Shatt al Arab. The problem of dissident Kurds fighting for their freedom also continued. In 1969 Kurds had attacked the government's oil refinery at Kirkuk. After this the government of Iran, seeing an opportunity to harass Iraq, began to supply Kurdish guerrillas with weapons. By 1974 a full-scale war existed between the Iraqi government and the Kurds, who controlled the mountainous areas in the north.

In March of 1975, Iraq and Iran settled the Shatt al Arab issue. Iran received the border it wanted; in return, the **shah** agreed to stop supporting the Kurds. Without weapons and an escape route into Iran, Kurdish resistance evaporated. To prevent further rebellions, the Iraqi government literally yanked more than 50,000 Kurds from their homes and moved them into empty areas, giving them tents to live in. They were threatened with death if they tried to return to the Kurdistan region. Al-Bakr's government then encouraged Arab Iraqis to move into the former homes of the Kurds in order to dilute the influence of the Kurdish population.

By the end of 1975, Saddam Hussein had clearly become one of the most powerful men in Iraq. While al-Bakr was considered the more respectable face of the government, he had become little more than a figurehead. Saddam was the regime's strongman, intimidating Iraqis to ensure that no one opposed the Baath Party. Political activity among civilians or within the army, aside from that connected to the Baath Party, was outlawed and could be punished by death.

SADDAM HUSSEIN TAKES POWER

In July 1979 Saddam Hussein, then vice president of Iraq, announced that he had discovered a plot to take over the government. Among the plotters, he claimed, were high-ranking members of Iraq's government; not only were they "traitors" to their friends, Saddam said, but they also were closely allied with Syria. Over the next two weeks, dozens of government officials and accused traitors were executed. President al-Bakr quietly slipped from the political scene, claiming ill health.

Saddam's authority soon became total. The people who were loyal to him were promoted to powerful positions in the government. In exchange, they agreed with him and supported his power grab. Saddam's most trusted officials were those who came from his hometown, Tikrit, and were members of his own family or tribe.

Saddam dealt strongly with any opposition. When Shiite Muslim religious leaders in southern Iraq encouraged resistance to the government, Saddam had some leading clerics killed and many others arrested. He accused numerous Shiites of supporting Iraq's rival, Iran, and thousands were forced to leave the country and move into Iran. After their deportation, their homes and belongings were sold.

Saddam had reason to be concerned about affairs in Iran. The pro-Western government of the shah had been overthrown in early 1979 by supporters of the radical Shiite cleric Ayatollah Ruhollah Khomeini. Khomeini had instituted a theocratic Shiite Muslim government. In the wake of Iran's Islamic Revolution, he encouraged Shiites in other countries to revolt against their leaders. Saddam Hussein's concern about the loyalty of his own Shiite population was warranted—he had ruthlessly oppressed the Shiites. Even before the Baath Party came to power, however, Shiites had been second-class citizens in Iraq, and they resented repression by the country's secular governments.

Saddam Hussein rose through the ranks of the Baath Party, finally seizing absolute power in July 1979 with a chilling, videotaped purge of party members.

The Sunni-Shiite split was not the only dimension to the animosity between Iran and Iraq. The people of Mesopotamia had been at odds with the many Persian peoples to their east for millennia. And there was a personal element as well—Khomeini hated Saddam Hussein and his secular regime, while Saddam detested the ayatollah and his theocratic rule. Perhaps most important, though, was Saddam's desire to make Iraq the leading power in the Middle East, which would require that it overcome its larger rival Iran. The Islamic Revolution had caused great unrest in Iran, and Saddam wanted to exploit what he perceived as a strategic moment of Iranian weakness.

He used the long-running Shatt al Arab dispute as an excuse to start a war. In September 1980, Saddam announced Iraq's claim to the entire waterway, and within a few days Iraqi troops had invaded Iran and captured some territory.

The Iran-Iraq War lasted for eight years, during which time neither side was able to make permanent or significant gains. Instead, the war devastated both countries. Each bombed the other's oil refineries; Iraq's oil revenues fell from $26 billion in 1980 to $9 billion in 1982. To pay for the war, Saddam borrowed billions of dollars from Arab countries, particularly Kuwait and Saudi Arabia.

The United States also provided crucial support to Iraq throughout the war. Under Khomeini's leadership Iran had become the mortal enemy of the United States, and President Ronald Reagan feared that if Iran defeated Iraq, the Islamic Revolution would spread into the Arab world. This might cut off access to the oil reserves of the Persian Gulf, which the Western economies needed. As a result, the U.S. government provided financial aid and training to the Iraqis, as well as information on Iranian military positions. (However, during the later years of the war, the Reagan administration arranged secret shipments of weapons to Iran, in exchange for Tehran's cooperation in freeing Western hostages being held in Lebanon by Iranian-supported groups.)

The Iran-Iraq War was an uncommonly merciless conflict, producing casualties estimated at more than a million people—and the two countries' combined population was under 80 million. But beyond the massive casualties, there was another disturbing development: the use of chemical weapons. In violation of the 1925 Geneva Protocol on the Use of Chemical Weapons—to which Iraq was a signatory—Saddam's forces on various occasions resorted to chemical warfare against their Iranian enemies. A 1986 report from the United Nations documented Iraq's use of the banned weapons, such as mustard gas and nerve gas; a separate British report released later that year estimated that at least 10,000 Iranian soldiers had been killed in Iraqi chemical attacks.

But Iraq's use of chemical warfare was not limited to attacks on enemy soldiers. In March 1988, a chemical attack by Saddam's forces killed some 5,000 Kurdish civilians in the village of Halabja. At the time, the Iraqis were recapturing Kurdish territory in north- eastern Iraq that had been occupied by Iranian troops.

The Halabja massacre was only the most famous chemical attack on the Kurds, but there were many others. The Kurds, who had always resisted the government of Iraq, had supported Iran's invasion of northern Iraq. After the Iranian army was forced from Iraq, Saddam enacted a brutal campaign against the entire Kurdish population. Any Kurd thought to be a guerrilla or a supporter of Iran was killed. Villages were totally destroyed and their survivors sent to camps set up by the government. Mustard gas and nerve gas were used on 67 Kurdish villages. Many of those who survived the gas attacks were badly injured and horribly deformed, and the countryside was seriously contaminated. In all, it is believed that 80 percent of the villages in the Kurdish area were destroyed and 60,000 people killed in this purge.

After eight long years, the Iran-Iraq War finally ended in August 1988 with a United Nations–sponsored cease-fire. Though Iran had sustained heavier casualties, Iraq, too, was devastated by the war its leader had started. Approximately 375,000 Iraqis had been killed or wounded, and 60,000 more had been captured. Economic losses were also staggering: cities, oil fields, and refineries had been wrecked, and many areas of the country were in ruins. By the end of the war Iraq owed about $80 billion, mostly to its Arab neighbors.

In the postwar period, half of Iraq's oil revenues were spent just to repay the country's war debt. Because Saddam needed huge amounts of money to rebuild his country, he turned to the Organization of Petroleum Exporting Countries (OPEC) for help. OPEC, made up of 11 countries that are among the largest global exporters of oil, is a cartel that attempts to control world oil prices by setting production quotas for its members. Saddam asked OPEC to grant Iraq a larger annual quota. By pumping more oil, Iraq would bring in more income, which would aid in the country's recovery. When OPEC refused Saddam's request, Iraq's leader demanded that Saudi Arabia and Kuwait cancel his debts, considering them grants instead. He argued that his war with Iran had been to defend the Arab world, and that they should participate in the cost. Both Saudi Arabia and Kuwait balked.

Saddam soon claimed that Kuwait was exceeding its OPEC quota, thereby lowering the price of oil, and also said that Kuwait was pumping oil from under Iraq's border. The dictator used these claims as a pretext to invade Kuwait on August 2, 1990. In less than a week, Saddam declared Kuwait the 19th province of Iraq. This would give Iraq greater access to the Persian Gulf, as well as control of Kuwait's rich oil fields.

The international community refused to accept the Iraqi takeover. The United Nations demanded that Iraq withdraw from the territory of its southern neighbor, and when Saddam did not respond, an international coalition put together by U.S. president George Bush went to war in January 1991 to liberate Kuwait. The Gulf War was relatively brief, and decidedly one-sided: Saddam's army was routed after a month of aerial bombardment and 100 hours of ground fighting. As defeated Iraqi troops retreated from Kuwait, they left a trail of devastation, setting fire to oil fields, looting homes, and destroying public buildings and infrastructure. The rebuilding of Kuwait would cost some $160 billion.

In the aftermath of the Gulf War, Shiite Muslims in the south and Kurds in the north—encouraged by the words of President George Bush—rebelled against Saddam's regime. In Shiite cities like Basra and Karbala, returning soldiers and Shiite civilians attacked government officials. If the rebels believed President Bush's call to overthrow Saddam meant that the United States would help them, however, they were wrong. And despite his colossal defeat in the Gulf War, Saddam had managed to preserve his best-trained and most loyal military force, the elite Republican Guard. The dictator sent Republican Guard units south to recapture the cities and put down the revolt. Thousands of Shiites were killed, and many more fled to Iran or to refugee camps set up by the U.S. military.

Next, the Republican Guard moved north to attack the Kurds. As Saddam's troops brutally crushed the Kurdish uprising, more than a million Kurds fled their homes and headed toward Turkey or Iran. These refugees faced harsh conditions, including scant supplies of food and water and inadequate shelter against the late-winter cold of Iraq's rugged mountains. Refugees began to die, and a massive humanitarian crisis loomed.

President George Bush greets U.S. troops in Saudi Arabia after the 1991 Gulf War. Although the brief war succeeded in expelling Iraq from Kuwait, it left Saddam Hussein in power.

After a period of hesitation, the United States, Britain, and France finally took action to protect the Kurds, setting up safe havens and declaring that no Iraqi aircraft would be permitted to fly north of the 36th parallel of latitude. This prevented Saddam's forces from using attack helicopters against the Kurds. A similar no-fly zone was later established south of the 33rd parallel, to give the Shiites a measure of protection.

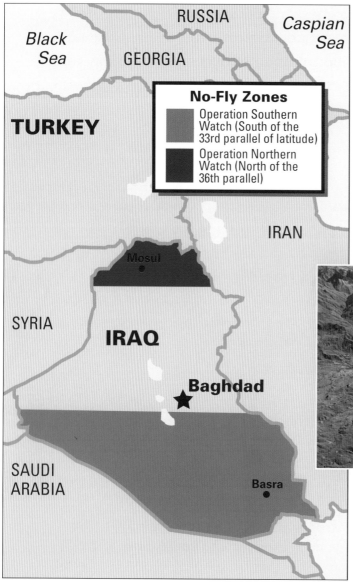

No-Fly Zones

Operation Southern Watch (South of the 33rd parallel of latitude)

Operation Northern Watch (North of the 36th parallel)

In the wake of Saddam's brutal suppression of the Kurdish and Shiite rebellions following the Gulf War, the United States and its coalition allies prevented Iraq from flying aircraft in the north and south of the country. Inset: A U.S. Air Force F-15C Eagle patrols the northern no-fly zone.

Protected from attack by U.S. and British fighter-jet patrols—which enforced the no-fly zone from 1991 until 2003—Kurds who had fled returned to their homes. The Kurds were even able to create an autonomous region in northern Iraq, where they enjoyed political freedom unknown in the rest of the country. Free elections were held in May of 1992, and in June of that year, an elected Kurdish Assembly convened for the first time.

THE EFFORT TO DISARM IRAQ

As part of the cease-fire that ended the 1991 Gulf War, Iraq agreed to United Nations resolutions demanding that it recognize the sovereignty of Kuwait and destroy its weapons of mass destruction. In addition to chemical weapons—which it had used during the war with Iran—Iraq had produced biological weapons, including munitions filled with concentrated anthrax and botulinum toxin. Even more alarming was Iraq's nuclear weapons program. Although it had signed the 1968 Treaty on the Non-Proliferation of Nuclear Weapons, Iraq had secretly been working on a nuclear bomb, perhaps since the early 1980s.

In early June of 1991, the United Nations Special Commission on Disarmament (UNSCOM) began searching Iraq for weapons of mass destruction. UNSCOM inspectors found and destroyed chemical weapons and proscribed missiles. They also concluded that Saddam's scientists had been considerably closer to developing nuclear weapons than Western intelligence analysts had suspected.

By late 1994, UNSCOM believed it was close to finishing its work. However, rumors emerged that Iraq had an undeclared biological weapons program, something that the country's leaders acknowledged in July 1995. The next month, Saddam's son-in-law, Hussein Kamil, who had been in charge of Iraq's proscribed weapons programs, defected. As a result of Kamil's defection, UNSCOM learned that Iraq had retained significant amounts of chemical agents, along with some missiles and other delivery systems. Iraq, however, never turned over any of that material. The Iraqis claimed they had destroyed it unilaterally, even though the U.N. cease-fire resolution called for UNSCOM to supervise destruction of that material.

Short of another full-scale war to remove Saddam Hussein from power—a course of action that lacked broad international support—the options for convincing Iraq to disarm were fairly limited. One option was the periodic bombing of selected targets. Another was continuation of the economic sanctions that the U.N. had imposed after Iraq's invasion of Kuwait. In theory, restricting Iraq's trade with other countries would not only pressure Saddam to comply with the disarmament requirements but also, if he resisted, limit his ability to rebuild his military and weapons programs.

Because Iraqi compliance was judged to be insufficient, the sanctions stayed in effect throughout the 1990s. Some world leaders found this troubling, because while Saddam's regime continued to enjoy sufficient resources to maintain its hold on power, ordinary Iraqis were suffering. Shortages of food and medicine caused misery and death. In response to this situation, the United Nations in 1995 established the oil-for-food program, which permitted Iraq to sell oil under U.N. supervision; most of the profits were supposed to go to the humanitarian needs of Iraq's people. But by most accounts the regime managed to divert oil-for-food money for its own use, and Iraqis continued to suffer. Anupama Rao Singh, head of the UNICEF office in Baghdad, commented on how Iraq's children had been affected. "What we found," Singh said, after a 1999 survey, "was that mortality rates in the south and center of Iraq for children under 5 years of age had more than doubled . . . which means that in practical terms one in ten children do not survive beyond their first birthday."

Throughout the 1990s, Saddam Hussein bedeviled U.S. policymakers. President Bill Clinton, who took office in 1993, pursued a policy of containment. The hope was that if Saddam could not be removed, he could at least be isolated and held in check through continued application of the economic sanctions. On occasion, however, the Clinton administration resorted to air strikes on Iraq. In June 1993, for example, President Clinton ordered a cruise missile attack on the office of Iraq's intelligence agency in Baghdad following revelations of an Iraqi plot to assassinate his predecessor, George Bush. Saddam's moves against the opposition Iraqi National Congress in 1996 provoked another cruise missile strike.

But for U.S. policymakers, uncertainty about Iraq's weapons programs was the greatest concern. In 1994 UNSCOM believed it was close to bringing Iraq into compliance with Resolution 687 (by which Iraq was supposed to give up all its weapons of mass destruction). Then Saddam Hussein's son-in-law, Hussein Kamel, defected to the West in 1995. He provided new information about Iraq's programs to build weapons of mass destruction. Soon, Iraq turned over information related to the country's nuclear, biological, and chemical weapons programs—computer files, photographs, documents, and memos.

At different times throughout 1996 and 1997, efforts by UNSCOM inspectors to inspect various sites in Iraq were blocked or delayed, resulting in several U.N. declarations of noncompliance with security council resolutions. In September 1998, Saddam Hussein demanded that American members of UNSCOM had to leave the country, accusing them of spying. In response the United Nations withdrew the entire team, and President Clinton sent U.S. Navy warships into the Persian Gulf, threatening Iraq with air strikes. Cornered, Saddam permitted the inspectors to return.

The dictator used many methods to frustrate UNSCOM's inspection efforts. Saddam declared his presidential palaces—some of which were huge compounds where just about anything could be hidden—off-limits to inspectors. He refused to allow UNSCOM to return to sites it had previously inspected. UNSCOM was prohibited from searching the headquarters of the Baath Party in Baghdad. Roadblocks were set up to keep the inspectors from reaching suspected weapons facilities.

In December 1998, with military action against Iraq imminent, the United Nations withdrew its inspectors. The United States and Great Britain then began Operation Desert Fox, a bombing campaign to force Saddam to comply with the U.N. resolutions. During the three-day operation, missiles were fired at strategic Iraqi military targets and suspected weapons sites. However, U.N. inspectors were not permitted to return to Iraq after this attack.

In the aftermath of the September 11, 2001, terrorist attacks against the United States, the U.S. government revised its policy toward Iraq, replacing "containment" with "regime change." President George W. Bush, who had taken office in January 2001,

U.N. weapons inspectors overseeing the disarmament of Iraq believed they were nearing completion of their task until the 1995 defection of Saddam Hussein's son-in-law Hussein Kamel. A member of Saddam's inner circle, Kamel revealed details about Iraq's illegal weapons programs. In 1996 Kamel returned to Iraq under Saddam's guarantee of safety, but the Iraqi dictator promptly killed him, along with his brother, his father, and his sister and her children.

and key members of his administration argued that the United Nations would become "irrelevant" if it did not respond to Saddam Hussein's continued flouting of its many resolutions regarding disarmament—16 resolutions since the 1991 Gulf War, according to the White House's count.

In November 2002, the United Nations Security Council voted unanimously to adopt Resolution 1441. The resolution gave Iraq "a final opportunity to comply with its disarmament obligations" and warned of "serious consequences" if it did not do so. Faced with the prospect of war, Saddam permitted U.N. weapons inspectors to return to Iraq in December.

Over the next few months, the Bush administration pressured other nations to find that Iraq was still in "material breach" of its obligations under Resolution 1441. Countries such as France, Germany, Russia, and China resisted, saying that the inspectors needed more time to work; the United States and its allies countered that Iraq was continuing its efforts to deceive inspectors.

On March 20, 2003, the United States and Great Britain began a war to drive Saddam from power. On April 7, American troops swept into Baghdad, and within two days it was apparent that the Iraqi regime had collapsed. As the military operations wound down, planners began to turn their attention to the task of creating a new government in Iraq—one they hoped would become the first democracy in the Arab world.

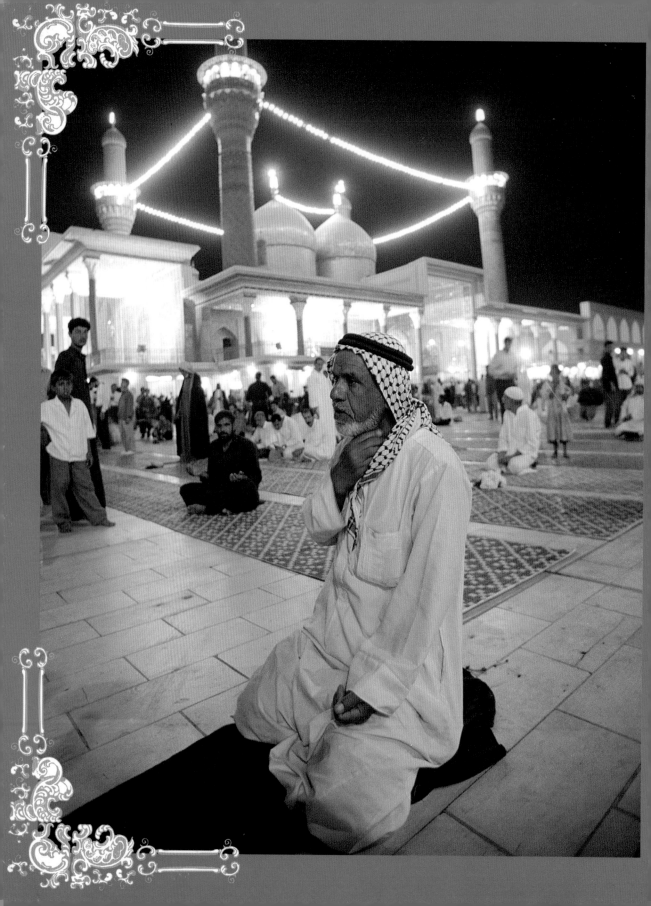

An Iraqi Muslim faces the holy city of Mecca to pray. About 97 percent of Iraq's people are adherents of Islam, the majority belonging to the Shia branch of the faith.

Religion, Politics, and the Economy

It is impossible to understand Iraq without understanding the country's most important religion, Islam. The Islamic faith is a vital part of everything Iraqis do. Islam is the world's second-largest religion; there are more than a billion Muslims, and many of them live in the Middle East and Asia. In Iraq, almost 97 percent of the people are Muslim.

ISLAM

The name of this **monotheistic** religion, Islam, comes from the Arabic verb *aslama*, which means "to surrender." Muslims, or followers of Islam, are those who surrender to the will of Allah, who is considered the one true God. Muslims believe that in the seventh century A.D., Allah spoke through the Angel Gabriel to Muhammad. Over a period of 22 years, the Prophet, as Muhammad is called, received Allah's messages and taught them to his followers. At first his disciples memorized them; they later wrote down the messages in a collection called the Qur'an (or Koran). The word *Qur'an* means "recitation" and comes from the Arabic word *iqira*, meaning "recite"—the first word that the Angel Gabriel spoke to Muhammad. Muslims believe the Qur'an is the perfect word of God.

Muslims are expected to follow five important precepts, or "pillars." The first is *shahada* ("testimony"), a prayer that expresses the belief at the heart of Islam: "There is no God but Allah, and Muhammad is the messenger of Allah." Devout Muslims recite the *shahada* each day. The second pillar is *salah* ("prayer"). Adult Muslims are required to pray five times during the day. The third pillar is *zakat* ("charity"), a donation given to people in need. The fourth pillar is *sawm* ("fasting"), a requirement that Muslims abstain from food, drink, and certain other activities during daylight hours of Ramadan, the ninth month of the lunar Islamic calendar. The fifth pillar is *hajj* ("pilgrimage"), a journey that Muslims who are physically and financially able must make to Mecca and other important Islamic sites at least once during their lifetime.

There are many sects of Islam, although the major split is between the Sunni Muslims and the Shiite Muslims. This division occurred more than 1,300 years ago, and the area of Iraq was a key battleground as Sunnis and Shiites fought for control of the religion. Today, it is estimated that more than 80 percent of the world's Muslims are Sunnis, while about 15 percent are Shiites. Iraq is one of just a few countries where the Shiite population is larger than the Sunni population. (Other Middle Eastern countries with more Shiites than Sunnis include Iran, Lebanon, and Bahrain.) According to recent figures, between 60 and 65 percent of Iraq's population are Shiites, while 32 to 37 percent are Sunnis. Despite the Shiites' majority status, since the time of the Ottoman Empire Sunni Muslims have traditionally held the power in Iraq.

In addition to the Qur'an, Muslims believe that the *hadiths* (sayings of the Prophet) are very important. The *hadiths* and stories about Muhammad are collected in the *Sunna* (traditions of the Prophet). Over the years, the Qur'an and the *Sunna* have given rise to a number of religious laws and codes of conduct; Islamic law is known as *Sharia*. In many Muslim countries of the Middle East, *Sharia* forms the basis not just for the justice system but also for legislation. While Iraq during the rule of Saddam Hussein had some special religious courts whose decisions were based on *Sharia*, the Baath Party was a secular organization, and Islam was not the foundation of the country's laws or justice system. (Unfortunately, legislation and the justice system were all too often simply tools for Saddam's regime to maintain its grip on power.)

OTHER RELIGIONS IN IRAQ

Although the overwhelming majority of Iraqis—both Arabs and Kurds—follow Islam, Iraq also has a small Christian community. Ancestors of these people have lived in Iraq for nearly 2,000 years. The Assyrians live in the northern part of Iraq, near the Kurdish enclaves that were protected by the northern no-fly zone between 1991 and 2003. Assyrians are a separate ethnic group from Kurds and Arabs. They still speak a version of Aramaic, the ancient language of the Middle East that was supplanted by Arabic during the spread of Islam in the seventh and eighth centuries. Historically, the Assyrians have been subject to repression by Iraqi rulers, and in recent years there have been some incidents of violence between Kurdish Muslims and Assyrian Christians. The Assyrian Christian population in Iraq is estimated at between 600,000 and 1 million.

THE GOVERNMENT OF IRAQ

Until U.S. and British forces invaded Iraq in 2003, the country was essentially a police state. At the top of the government pyramid was the Revolutionary Command Council (RCC), a group of eight men chosen by the Regional Command of the Baath Party. The RCC acted as both the executive and legislative branches of the government—in other words, it made the laws and carried them out. Saddam Hussein officially became chairman of the RCC, and therefore president of Iraq and commander-in-chief of its military, in 1979, although he held a great deal of power for many years before that.

According to Iraq's 1970 constitution, laws made by the Revolutionary Command Council were supposed to be sent to a 250-member National Assembly (Majlis al-Watani) for approval. However, only approved Baath Party candidates could be elected to the National Assembly, and it had no real authority anyway. Judges were appointed by Saddam Hussein and controlled by the RCC.

Before the fall of Saddam's regime, more than 400,000 Iraqis were in the armed forces. This was less than half the size of the Iraqi military at the start of the 1991 Gulf War, but it still ranked as the second-largest armed force in the Arab world, behind only Egypt. The core of the Iraqi military was the Republican Guard, which consisted of approximately 150,000 well-trained and well-equipped soldiers. Many of these soldiers came from the area around Saddam's hometown, Tikrit; during his rule they were given special privileges and thus had a special loyalty to the dictator.

One of the most feared organizations in Iraq was the Mukhabarat, or secret police. Its main purpose was to protect the Baath Party and its officials and to enforce government policies. Saddam Hussein used the Mukhabarat to gather intelligence against his enemies, and to intimidate and control the population and repress any dissent.

With the fall of Saddam Hussein's regime in the spring of 2003, the United States and Great Britain hoped to work with Iraqis to create a democratic government. The plan was to set up a transitional

A television image shows Saddam Hussein meeting with his cabinet, September 25, 2002. Although Iraq had some of the trappings of democracy, including elections and a legislative assembly, Saddam actually wielded absolute power.

authority, under the auspices of U.S. officials, before the eventual establishment of a freely elected Iraqi government. About 250 Iraqi leaders were brought together on April 28, 2003, for a meeting to discuss the future of their country. British Foreign Office minister Mike O'Brien, who attended the meeting, voiced the view that Iraqis should vote in a national referendum on a new constitution before electing their own government. "I hope we then move to a constitutional assembly, then a referendum and a new constitution and then a directly and properly elected democratic government of Iraq," he said.

THE ECONOMY OF IRAQ

When Marco Polo visited the Mesopotamia region during his travels in the 13th century, he saw the commodity that would become the foundation of Iraq's economy. "There is a fountain of oil,

A group of oil-field workers preparing to take a municipal bus to the oil fields.

which discharges so great a quantity as to furnish loading for camels," Polo wrote in his famous book. "It is good for burning. In the neighboring country no other is used in their lamps, and people come from distant parts to procure it."

Today, the production of oil is the most important part of Iraq's economy. Iraq has more than 112 billion barrels of proven oil reserves, giving it the second-largest reserves of any country in the world. Some oil industry experts believe that a huge amount of oil—possibly as much as another 220 billion barrels—may still lie hidden beneath Iraq's sands. The oil flows from 70 oil fields throughout the country, from Kirkuk in the northeast to Basra in the south.

Iraq has nine oil refineries. The two largest are in central Iraq—one at Bayji, which is north of Baghdad, and another, called Dawrah, in Baghdad.

Iraq fully nationalized the oil industry in 1975, and by 1979 it was producing 3.4 million barrels per day (bpd). Production dropped off during the Iran-Iraq War (1980–88), but by 1989 Iraq had rebuilt its extraction and refining capability and was nearly back to the 1979 production level.

After Iraq's invasion of Kuwait and the Gulf War, oil production fell to less than 600,000 bpd, due in large part to the United Nations sanctions against the country. As Iraq was permitted to export greater amounts of oil through the U.N.'s oil-for-food program, production gradually increased, officially reaching about 2 million bpd during 2001. Actual production is a harder number to pin down, as it is believed that Iraq illegally smuggled out oil through various routes.

In addition to its vast oil resources, Iraq has 110 trillion cubic feet of proven natural gas reserves. Of that, 70 percent is "associated"

An oil pumping station in southern Iraq. The country controls the world's second-largest petroleum reserves, and oil is an important part of Iraq's economy.

natural gas, which is produced at the same time that oil is extracted.

Sulfur and phosphate are also plentiful in Iraq. One of the largest deposits of sulfur in the world is mined at Mishraq, just south of Mosul. Phosphate is mined at Akashat on the Euphrates River near the Syrian border.

There are three main manufacturing areas in Iraq, the most important of which is near Baghdad. Another one is at Basra, to the south of Baghdad. The third is in a triangle formed by the northern cities of Mosul, Irbil, and Kirkuk. Pharmaceuticals, paper and plastic products, household appliances, clothing, and automobiles are produced in all three regions. In addition, for generations Mosul has been an important textile center.

Although Mesopotamia is known as an early center of agriculture, farming plays only a small part in modern Iraq's economy, con-

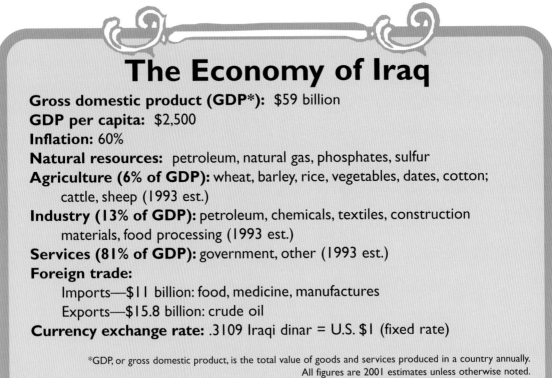

The Economy of Iraq

Gross domestic product (GDP*): $59 billion
GDP per capita: $2,500
Inflation: 60%
Natural resources: petroleum, natural gas, phosphates, sulfur
Agriculture (6% of GDP): wheat, barley, rice, vegetables, dates, cotton; cattle, sheep (1993 est.)
Industry (13% of GDP): petroleum, chemicals, textiles, construction materials, food processing (1993 est.)
Services (81% of GDP): government, other (1993 est.)
Foreign trade:
  Imports—$11 billion: food, medicine, manufactures
  Exports—$15.8 billion: crude oil
Currency exchange rate: .3109 Iraqi dinar = U.S. $1 (fixed rate)

*GDP, or gross domestic product, is the total value of goods and services produced in a country annually.
All figures are 2001 estimates unless otherwise noted.
Source: CIA World Factbook, 2002.

tributing just 6 percent to the country's gross domestic product. Only about 13 percent of Iraq is fit for growing crops, and about half of that land is in the Kurdish areas of the north and northeast, where rain waters the land. Most of the farm products are produced on the plains of central Iraq, where fields are watered by irrigation—just as they have been since the time of the Sumerians. This dependence on irrigation in the central region makes Turkish and Syrian water projects on the Euphrates River a very serious issue to the people of Iraq.

Another serious issue affecting agriculture in Iraq is **salinity**. The high water table in Iraq, the land's poor drainage, and the high rate of evaporation caused by the region's high temperatures cause salt to build up near the surface of the ground. The increasing salt level gradually makes it impossible to grow crops, turning the land into desert. Today, salinity affects almost two-thirds of Iraq, and it has caused once-productive land to be abandoned. In recent years, projects have been started to reclaim this land and make it useful again. However, this is a long, difficult process that requires consistent effort.

The major farm crops of Iraq include barley and wheat, which are grown during the winter, and cotton, potatoes, and millet, which are grown in the summer. Other summer crops include sorghum and tobacco. Dates and rice grow in the irrigated areas of the central plains along the rivers and canals.

Iraqi women protest the United Nations—imposed trade sanctions, 1993. With respect to the status of women, Iraq has been fairly liberal, at least in comparison with some of the other Arab countries. In 1970, for example, Iraq's constitution was changed to guarantee women equal treatment with men under the law.

The People

$\mathcal{A}$rab culture came to dominate Iraq after the Muslim conquests of the seventh and eighth centuries. Today, almost 8 in 10 of Iraq's approximately 24 million people are of Arab ancestry. Most of these Arabs are Shiite Muslims, who live predominantly in the southern or central parts of the country.

Iraq's second-largest ethnic group is its approximately 4.5 million Kurds, who make up about 19 percent of the population. Most of the Kurdish population is located in the northern part of Iraq. The Kurds' language and culture differs greatly from that of Arab Iraqis. Also, most of the Kurds are Sunni Muslims, unlike the Shiite Arab majority.

The Kurds have been called the largest ethnic group without their own state. There are estimated to be about 25 million Kurds worldwide; most of them live in an area known as Kurdistan, which includes parts of present-day Iraq, Iran, Turkey, and Syria. Since the early years of the 20th century,

> Kurds living in the mountains wear turbans called *mishki*, baggy trousers called *sharwal*, and short jackets with a waistband of many colors and patterns. They sometimes carry daggers in their waistbands.

many Kurds have campaigned for their own independent state in this region. However, all of the governments that would be affected oppose giving up some of their territory for a Kurdish state.

After the 1991 Gulf War, the United States and Great Britain imposed a no-fly zone over northern Iraq to protect the Kurds from Saddam Hussein's armies. With this protection, Iraqi Kurdistan became a de facto democratic state during the 1990s; its people elected a lawmaking parliament, developed a system of government, and established an army and police force.

Yet the Kurdistan model proved far from perfect. Two rival groups, the Kurdistan Democratic Party and the Patriotic Union of Kurdistan, battled for control. Their political fighting at times turned into actual violence. Kurds have also attempted to terrorize and control the Assyrian Christian population living in the northern provinces of Iraq.

The Assyrians make up about 1 percent of Iraq's total population. Other ethnic groups living in the country include Turkomen, a nomadic Turkic people who live along the northern border of Iraq and make up about 1.4 percent of the total population. Armenians, Persians, and smaller groups together make up less than 2 percent of Iraq's population.

Wars and sanctions have affected population growth in Iraq. During the 1980s, the country's population growth rate was 3.2 percent per year, but by the early 1990s the figure had slipped below 2 percent per year as the country's birth rate dropped. By 2002 the population growth rate had risen to 2.82 percent.

Iraq's largest concentration of people is in Bagdad—home to nearly one in four Iraqis—and a narrow strip running southeast of the capital along the Tigris River. Few people live west of the Euphrates.

The U.N. sanctions have had a very negative effect on the people of Iraq. In 1997 UNICEF estimated that 1.2 million Iraqis had died prematurely as a result of the sanctions, and an August 1999 UNICEF survey showed that the mortality rate for children under age 5 had risen from 56 deaths per 1,000 births (1984–89) to 131 deaths per 1,000 births (1994–99). During that time malnourishment became a widespread problem among children in Iraq.

An Iraqi family eats a meal together. For Iraqis, like other Arabs, maintaining strong ties with family is imperative.

FAMILY LIFE IN IRAQ

The role of family in the Arab world helps explain much about the Arab Iraqi people. Kinship groups are the basic units in Iraqi society. Iraqis show their greatest loyalty to their immediate family and extended family. Usually three generations live together and ʾre their lives, each having clear responsibilities. Other relatives lose by in the neighborhood. Often members of the same d family are in business together because of the trust and ʾond built up among them. A common proverb among

Arabs is "I and my brothers against my cousin; I and my cousin against the stranger (or the world)."

One family is usually made up of an older couple, their sons, daughters-in-law, and their grandchildren. Traditionally, daughters remain in the home until they marry. Then they move into the home of their husband's family. Sometimes other relatives also might be a part of the household. The oldest male in that family is the head of the whole family and has the final word on all decisions. The father metes out the punishment, which can be severe, while the mother tends to offer the love and compassion. As in other Arab countries, Iraq's is a highly **patriarchal** society in which the male dominates, and male children are highly prized.

In spite of changing times, in many families the father decides the activities of the members under him, even determining what jobs his sons will have. Along with his wife, the father will pick out a husband for their daughter. Marriage is much more of a contract between two groups than the personal choice of two people, because the marriage will affect each of the families involved.

Iraqis, like other Arabs, have a special love for the Arabic language. Since they believe the Qur'an represents the actual words of God, and since it was given to Muhammad in the Arabic language, it follows, then, that the original, classic Arabic is a divine language, according to devout Muslims. There are different Arabic **dialects**, however. Many say that Arabic can only be compared to music in the effect it has on those who speak and listen to it. In *The Arab Mind* Philip Hitti, a leading Arab-American historian, was quoted as saying, "Hardly any language seems capable of exercising over the minds of its users such influence as Arabic. Modern

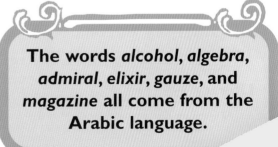

The words *alcohol, algebra, admiral, elixir, gauze,* and *magazine* all come from the Arabic language.

audiences in Baghdad, Damascus and Cairo can be stirred to the highest degree by the recital of poems only vaguely comprehended, and by the delivery of orations in the classical tongue, though only partially understood."

Traditionally, Kurds have been organized by tribes, although tribal affiliation has become less important in recent years. Kurdish villages and cities have grown in the highlands and mountain valleys of northern Iraq, particularly in the three provinces of As Sulaymaniyah, Irbil, and Dahuk.

The Kurds have their own traditions and cultures. One source of pride that unifies Kurds is their language. With the growth of Iraqi Kurdistan, school lessons began to be taught in Kurdish, rather than in Arabic.

THE ARTS

Islamic tradition forbids visual art in which Allah or living people are represented. As a result, throughout history Arab artists have expressed themselves through decorative art.

One art form popular in Iraq is **calligraphy**, writing so beautiful that it becomes a

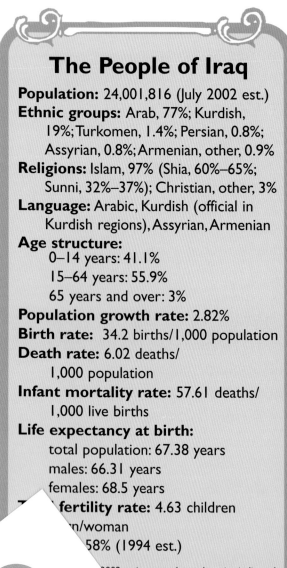

The People of Iraq

Population: 24,001,816 (July 2002 est.)
Ethnic groups: Arab, 77%; Kurdish, 19%; Turkomen, 1.4%; Persian, 0.8%; Assyrian, 0.8%; Armenian, other, 0.9%
Religions: Islam, 97% (Shia, 60%–65%; Sunni, 32%–37%); Christian, other, 3%
Language: Arabic, Kurdish (official in Kurdish regions), Assyrian, Armenian
Age structure:
　0–14 years: 41.1%
　15–64 years: 55.9%
　65 years and over: 3%
Population growth rate: 2.82%
Birth rate: 34.2 births/1,000 population
Death rate: 6.02 deaths/ 1,000 population
Infant mortality rate: 57.61 deaths/ 1,000 live births
Life expectancy at birth:
　total population: 67.38 years
　males: 66.31 years
　females: 68.5 years
**　 fertility rate:** 4.63 children
　　n/woman
　　58% (1994 est.)

2002 estimates unless otherwise indicated. Adapted from CIA World Factbook, 2002.

work of art in itself. Calligraphy—often sections of the Qur'an or Arab proverbs—can be used to decorate everyday items made from paper, metal, or wood. Sometimes the writing is so ornate that it is difficult to make out the exact words, and the calligraphy must be examined carefully in order to decipher the message.

Creating intricate **geometric** designs is another form of Iraqi art. The artist begins with a simple geometric form, such as a square, a circle, or a **polygon**, then uses this form to create complex patterns. Designs can be made with tile to decorate walls and doorways; colorful geometric designs can also be found on household items and clothing.

Islamic architecture is another creative art form. Though the Arabs created palaces and other private buildings, the most lasting are the mosques. In Baghdad the celebrated Al-Kadhimain Mosque, built in the 16th century, has gold-capped domes and minarets rising above a courtyard.

Music is an important part of life in Iraq. Singers are accompanied by musical instruments such as the oud, which is something like a guitar. Iraqi musicians also play *darabukkas* (drums), *duffs* (tambourines), stringed instruments called *rabaabs*, the *qarna* (a horn), and the *zummara* (a double flute).

Traditional Iraqi music differs from American music in that it has only a melody, whereas Western music incorporates both melody and harmony. To a Westerner, this traditional Iraqi music is **plaintive** and squealing, while to many Iraqis Western music sounds crude and rough. However, younger Iraqis enjoy popular Western music.

Literature is an art form that has existed in Iraq since ancient times. One of the oldest writings in the world is the *Epic of Gilgamesh*, the story of an ancient Mesopotamian king's adventures.

During the last decade of the 20th century and the early years of the 21st, many modern Iraqi artists fled their country, seeking

Geometric motifs and calligraphy adorn this Islamic shrine in the Iraqi town of Al-Kufa. Such forms of decoration are common because Islam traditionally forbids the depiction of humans.

asylum in the West as a result of political persecution. Poets and writers frequently have expressed their longing for Iraq in their work. An exhibition of modern Iraqi artists' work, presenting their responses to what has happened to their country, was held in Great Britain in 2001 and in the United States in 2002.

Iraq's archaeological heritage is among the richest in the entire world. Shown here are the remains of the Sassanid palace of Ctesiphon in Taq-i-Kisra.

Communities

Traditionally Iraq was a country of small farming communities, but that changed in the second half of the 20th century. According to a September 2002 study by the World Bank, 68 percent of Iraqis live in urban areas. The largest of these is Baghdad, the capital, with a population of approximately 5.8 million people. Other large cities in Iraq include Mosul (population: 1.8 million) and Basra (population: 1.4 million).

BAGHDAD

Baghdad was founded in A.D. 762 by Abu Jafar al-Mansur, the second Abbasid caliph. The city, originally built on the west bank of the Tigris River, was called Madinat as-Salam—"the City of Peace." Baghdad was the center of the Islamic world during the early decades of the Abbasid dynasty (750–1258), reaching its greatest level of prosperity in the ninth century.

The city was sacked by the Mongols during their 13th-century invasion. Though it was rebuilt, it would never regain its previous glory. After the region came under the control of the Ottoman Empire in the early part of the 16th century, Baghdad fell into decline.

When Iraq became an independent country in the early 20th century, Baghdad began to grow with a program of construction and modernization. This increased during the 1960s and 1970s, as wealth from the sale of oil began to flow into Iraq. However, Iraq's wars in the 1980s and after forced many projects to be postponed or cancelled. Allied bombing attacks during the 1991 Gulf War and the 2003 war turned parts of the city into rubble.

Baghdad sprawls across both banks of the Tigris River, covering an area of about 800 square miles (2,071 sq km). About one-quarter of Iraq's people live in or around the city. Much of Iraq's industry can be found near Baghdad, and Saddam Hussein's main presidential palace, which included the main government buildings, was located in the heart of Baghdad.

Iraq contains many mosques and Islamic shrines dating back more than 1,000 years. Perhaps the most famous is the ninth-century Great Shrine of al-Mutawakkil, located outside Baghdad. Its spiral minaret soars 164 feet (50 meters). Another landmark near Baghdad is the Arch of Ctesiphon, which is all that is left of a Persian city built 2,200 years ago. The arch is believed to be the widest single-span brick vault in the world.

MOSUL

The second-largest city in Iraq is Mosul, located in the northern part of the country near the Kurdish region. For thousands of years Mosul has been known for textile exports. More recently, it has become an important center for oil refining, because it is near Iraq's northern oil fields, which are among the richest in the world.

The modern city was built on the site of Nineveh, the administrative center of the ancient Assyrian Empire. This means that the Mosul area has been inhabited for more than 6,700 years.

Mosul was perhaps the most prosperous Iraqi city during the period of Ottoman rule (1534–1918), because of its proximity to Turkey. Today, the Turks believe they have a historical claim to the Mosul region. This has caused tensions between the northern Kurds, who wish to establish their own state, and Turkey, which has had problems with its own Kurdish minority.

In addition to the large Kurdish population living in and around Mosul, the city is also believed to have a larger Christian population than any other city in Iraq. One religious site is Nebi Yunus, a mosque that overlooks Mosul and is believed to contain the tomb of Jonah (in Arabic, Yunus), a prophet recognized by Jews, Christians, and Muslims.

The city of Tikrit, located near Mosul, is notable as the birthplace of both the 12th-century Islamic leader Saladin and Saddam Hussein.

BASRA

Basra, in southeastern Iraq, is the country's principal port and its third-largest city. It is located on the Shatt al Arab, about 75 miles (121 km) from the Persian Gulf. Basra is one of Iraq's oldest cities; it was founded in A.D. 636 by Caliph Umar I. It is located near an even older city—Ur, the ancient Sumerian city that flourished more than 4,000 years ago.

Because of Basra's proximity to southern Iraq's many oil fields, the city is an important center for petroleum production. Many refineries have been built in and around Basra.

During the Iran-Iraq War, the city was heavily contested because of its strategic location on the Shatt al Arab near the Iran border. Basra was also targeted during the 1991 Gulf War. After the war,

The ruins of the ancient Sumerian city of Ur are located near Basra. By the third millennium B.C., Ur was already flourishing as a center of trade and government.

Shiite Muslims in Basra started an uprising against Saddam Hussein's government, but their revolt was not supported by coalition troops, and Saddam's Republican Guard brutally restored order. After the revolt was quashed, Saddam refused to rebuild some parts of the ruined city.

In 2003 British forces captured Basra in the early days of the fighting to topple Saddam Hussein's regime.

OTHER IMPORTANT CITIES

Irbil (population 865,000) served as the capital of the semi-independent Iraqi Kurdistan after the 1991 Gulf War. It is an important commercial center in the region. Irbil was founded thousands of years ago by the Medes; it is located 50 miles (81 km) east of Mosul.

Kirkuk (population 756,000) is an important oil-producing center in northwestern Iraq. It is connected via pipeline to the Mediterranean Sea. The city's origins date back about 5,000 years. Most of the inhabitants of Kirkuk are Kurds. Kurkuk is 90 miles (145 km) southeast of Mosul.

The two most important religious cities in Iraq are Karbala and An Najaf. Both are located in central Iraq. Karbala is the place where the Shiite leader Hussein was killed in battle in A.D. 680. A beautiful shrine in Karbala reminds Shiite pilgrims of Hussein's martyrdom. The tomb of Ali, the fourth Islamic caliph and the father of Hussein, is located in a mosque in nearby An Najaf. Shiite Muslims consider these two cities to be as important as Mecca and Medina.

Two Iraqi boys pose beside a toppled statue of Saddam Hussein, April 14, 2003. Iraq's emergence from 24 years of ruthless rule under Saddam presented exciting possibilities—but also significant challenges.

Foreign Relations

In early April 2003, after just a few weeks of fighting, U.S. Marines helped a crowd of cheering Iraqis topple an enormous statue of Saddam Hussein in Baghdad. To many people around the world, this scene was a symbol of the toppling of Saddam Hussein's regime.

"Regime change" in Iraq had been a long-standing goal of President George W. Bush. Bush administration officials and their supporters expressed the hope that if Saddam's dictatorship fell, the United States could help build Iraq into a democracy—the first real democracy among the Arab states. And a successful, democratic Iraq, U.S. leaders said openly, might serve as a model for other Arab societies.

The early plan for postwar Iraq was for the creation of an interim government consisting of a council of leaders (numbering perhaps eight or nine) from various Iraqi groups. Under U.S. direction, this interim government would allow the

Jay Garner (left), a retired American general, was chosen to direct the Office of Reconstruction and Humanitarian Assistance for Post-War Iraq. His many responsibilities included facilitating the repair of Iraq's infrastructure, managing humanitarian relief, keeping the country's civil service functioning, and helping set up an interim government. In mid-May 2003 Garner was replaced by L. Paul Bremer (right), a former U.S. ambassador who was named administrator of the Coalition Provisional Authority in Iraq.

country to function while preparations for a democratic Iraqi government were under way. Iraqi schools, hospitals, police, and utility systems would operate under the direction of U.S. ministers. The United States intended to pay the salaries of Iraqi government officials and provide funds to keep government ministries operating.

The first step was an intense humanitarian effort to distribute food, water, and medicine. Initially, food would be provided by the United States, although the U.N. World Food Program was expected to oversee the national distribution network. A retired U.S. Army general, Jay M. Garner, was selected to oversee the humanitarian aid program and the interim government.

On April 28, 2003, Garner met with approximately 250 Iraqi political, economic, and religious leaders to discuss the shape of the new government of Iraq. The date was significant—it was the 66th birthday of Saddam Hussein, which until his overthrow had been a national holiday. "Today on the birthday of Saddam Hussein let us start the democratic process for the children of Iraq," Garner told the assembled Iraqi leaders, exhorting them to accept the responsibility of rebuilding their war-torn country.

With the overthrow of Saddam Hussein, groups that had long been suppressed, such as Shiites and Kurds, looked forward to gaining power in Iraq. However, as the United States promised to work toward building democracy in Iraq, it also warned Iraq's neighbors not to interfere with the reconstruction of the country. The warnings were particularly directed at its two largest neighbors, Iran and Turkey.

IRAQ, IRAN, AND TURKEY

Although Iraq shares borders with both Iran and Turkey, the people of these three countries are separated by ethnicity, language, and culture. Throughout history, the area of modern-day Iraq was ruled by both Persian dynasties and by the Ottoman Empire. As a result, there remains some resentment toward Iraq's neighbors.

In 1979 strong-willed leaders came to power in both Iran and Iraq. Saddam Hussein had been one of the most powerful members of Iraq's Baath Party for more than a decade, but he seized total control of the government in a bloody purge. At the same time, in Iran, the government of Shah Mohammad Reza Pahlavi was being shaken. The shah, whose regime was supported by the United

The Shiite cleric Ayatollah Ruhollah Khomeini became Iran's Supreme Leader in 1979. Khomeini's attempts to export radical Islamic fundamentalism contributed to Saddam Hussein's decision to launch a war against Iran the following year.

States, could not stop demonstrations and protests held throughout the country during much of 1978. When he fled Iran, a Shiite religious leader, Ayatollah Ruhollah Khomeini, seized power and established a theocratic state. The new Iranian government was very hostile toward the United States, which Khomeini called "the Great Satan."

The Iranian revolution posed a threat for Saddam Hussein and his secular dictatorship, particularly as Khomeini began to urge Shiites in other countries of the Middle East to rise up against their governments. Saddam feared that Iraq's majority Shiite population would join forces with Iran if the new theocracy were able to export its revolution.

There was a personal element as well. In 1964 Khomeini had been forced into exile from Iran; he settled in the Iraqi city of An

Najaf, an important Shiite religious center. However, during the 1978 unrest in Iran, the shah asked the Iraqi government to expel Khomeini, who was inciting the public uprisings. Saddam was happy to get rid of Khomeini. However, he could not have been happy to see this enemy become the leader of a neighboring nation with more than twice as many people as Iraq.

Saddam Hussein may have decided to go to war with Iran in 1980 because the new Iranian government was not yet stable, and he hoped to weaken or destroy Khomeini's power. The Iran-Iraq War devastated both countries. After eight years of fighting, neither side had made significant territorial gains, and Iraq's economy had nearly been ruined. Yet after the two countries agreed to peace terms set by the United Nations, Saddam Hussein often boasted of his "victory" over Iran. However, the only reason the war might be considered a victory for Iraq is that Iran was weakened and its government lost the support of some of its people because of the sufferings caused by the war.

During the 1990s, the governments of Iran and Iraq publicly pledged to improve relations. However, some problems have never been completely resolved, such as ownership of the Shatt al Arab. And in June 2002, Iraq protested to the United Nations about what it called breaches of the 1988 U.N. cease-fire, including attacks on Iraqi civilians by Iranian forces.

After Saddam Hussein's government was overthrown in 2003, reports began to circulate that Iranians had secretly entered southern Iraq and were organizing Shiite protests against the U.S. presence in Iraq. This raised fears that the new Iraqi government might become a strict Shiite theocracy like Iran's, rather than the democracy the United States had envisioned.

In response, U.S. president George W. Bush sent a message to Iranian leaders that outside interference by Iran during the reconstruction of Iraq would not be tolerated. At the same time, Secretary of Defense Donald Rumsfeld told reporters, "We will not allow the Iraqi people's democratic transition to be hijacked by those who might wish to install another form of dictatorship."

The government of Turkey was also intensely interested in developments within Iraq. Both Iraq and Turkey have Kurdish minorities, and Turkish officials have long sought to prevent the two groups from joining together to create a separate Kurdish state. For decades, the Turks have struggled to suppress Kurdish nationalism, and during the 1990s Turkish troops occasionally entered northern Iraq, hunting for Kurdish rebels fighting against the Turkish government.

During the 1990s, Turkey's close ties to the United States and Europe meant that the country's relations with Iraq were adversarial. Turkish airfields and other military facilities were used by U.S. warplanes patrolling the northern no-fly zone. And in 1991, during the Gulf War, Turkey closed an important oil pipeline that ran from Kirkuk to the Mediterranean Sea. That pipeline was reopened in 1997.

For its part, Iraq has been concerned about Turkey's use of water from the Tigris and Euphrates Rivers. Turkish water projects greatly affect the amount of water that Iraq can draw from those water resources.

IRAQ AND THE ARAB WORLD

Until the Gulf War, Iraq was a major force in the region mainly because of its military strength—as of 1991 it had the fourth-largest army in the entire world, with nearly one million active-duty soldiers. At various times Iraqi military strength has alarmed its Arab neighbors—Kuwait, Saudi Arabia, Jordan, and Syria—as some of Iraq's leaders have clearly indicated their desire to rule over a united Arab nation.

Historically, Iraqi leaders have considered Kuwait to be part of their territory. The tiny kingdom of Kuwait was founded in 1756. Although it was on the fringes of the Ottoman Empire in the 18th and 19th centuries, it was never really part of the empire. British influence was more prevalent than Turkish; in 1899 Kuwait became a British protectorate, and remained under British control until 1961, when it became an independent state.

Long before Iraq's 1990 invasion of Kuwait, the leaders of Iraq coveted Kuwait's oil wealth as well as its long coastline on the Persian Gulf. As early as 1940, King Ghazi of Iraq talked about making Kuwait part of his country. Later, when Abd al-Karim Qasim took over the reins of government in 1961, he claimed Kuwait for Iraq and threatened to invade—an invasion that was cancelled only after British warships and troops were rushed to the Gulf to protect Kuwait. When the Baath Party came to power in Iraq in 1963, it recognized the independence of Kuwait; a few years later, however, the Baath Party began to pressure Kuwait to become part of Iraq.

During the Iran-Iraq War, the government of Kuwait loaned $10 billion to Iraq. After the war had ended, however, Saddam Hussein said that Kuwait should consider the money a grant rather than a loan. Saddam's argument was that Iraq had protected Kuwait and the other Arab nations by fighting with Iran—an assertion that failed to convince many in the Arab world. Kuwait's refusal to write off the debt was one of the reasons Iraq invaded the country in August 1990. Even after coalition forces liberated Kuwait, Iraq was not required to repay the money, and the issue remained a source of friction between the two countries.

Another issue surrounds the disappearance of several hundred Kuwaiti citizens during Iraq's cruel seven-month-long occupation of its southern neighbor. Until its demise Saddam Hussein's government denied it knew anything about these 600 or more missing Kuwaitis.

After the Gulf War, the two Arab countries attempted to improve their frayed relations. In November 1994, Iraq gave up its claim to Kuwait and to the Bubiyan and Warbah islands when it formally accepted borders established by the United Nations. And in March 2002, Iraq signed an agreement with Kuwait in which it promised to respect the country's sovereignty. This agreement, negotiated through the diplomatic efforts of Qatar and Oman, occurred at an Arab League summit in Lebanon.

Iraq's relationship with Saudi Arabia has also undergone many changes. In the early 1970s, Iraq's leaders sometimes spoke out against the ruling family of Saudi Arabia. But in the years before Saddam Hussein seized total power, he began to cultivate a better

Jordan's King Hussein did not condemn Iraq's 1990 invasion of Kuwait but instead tried to steer a middle course between his large Arab neighbor and the nations of the West.

relationship with the Saudis. Crown Prince Fahd, who would later become king of Saudi Arabia, visited Saddam in Baghdad; Saddam paid a return visit to Fahd in Jedda, Saudi Arabia, the following year. When Saddam became president of Iraq, the Saudi government supported him, and when Iraq started its war against Iran in 1980, the Saudis were willing to provide financial assistance. Eventually, Saudi Arabia loaned Iraq almost $26 billion. However, when the war finally ended in 1988, Saddam refused to repay the loan, insisting—as he had with Kuwait—that it should be considered a grant, because Iraq had protected the Arab Gulf states from the danger of Iranian aggression.

After Saddam invaded Kuwait, Saudi Arabia's leaders feared their country would be next. The Saudi monarchy publicly opposed Iraq's occupation of Kuwait and permitted the international coalition to use bases on Saudi soil. Saudi Arabia was a key member of the coalition. More than half a million soldiers were assembled on Saudi territory, and the attack on Iraq came from Saudi Arabia. The government also shut down an oil pipeline from Iraq that had been built in 1985, a move that constricted Iraq's economy.

Relations between Saudi Arabia and Iraq remained uneasy after the end of the 1991 Gulf War. However, when the United States was making its preparations to attack Iraq in late 2002 and early 2003, the Saudis refused to allow bases in their country to be used for the war against Saddam Hussein's regime.

Jordan was one of the few countries that did not condemn Iraq's 1990 invasion of Kuwait. Jordan's King Hussein made this decision in part because of fears about the stability of his own government. Jordan, which also borders Israel, has a large population of Palestinian Arabs. The Palestinians overwhelmingly supported Saddam Hussein, and the king was concerned that they might revolt and overthrow his monarchy if he joined the U.S.-led coalition against Iraq.

President George W. Bush (left) and Secretary of Defense Donald Rumsfeld, two of the architects of the war to topple Saddam Hussein, hoped that the establishment of a democratic Iraq would lead to wide-ranging reforms among the Arab regimes of the Middle East.

Because Jordan is small, it has tried to maintain good relations with all of its neighbors. While Iraq was under international sanctions, Jordan received lucrative contracts to provide food in exchange for Iraqi oil. In November 2000 Jordan's prime minister visited Baghdad, becoming the first leading member of an Arab government to visit Iraq since the imposition of the sanctions.

Syria, Iraq's neighbor to the northeast, has had uneven relations with Baghdad over the years. Although Syria's government is a Baath Party–controlled dictatorship, like Iraq's before the fall of Saddam Hussein, the governments of the two countries have often disagreed. Syria is also an ally of Iran, the enemy of Iraq during

Saddam's rule. During the 1991 Gulf War, Syria was a member of the international coalition that ousted Iraq from Kuwait, and relations officially remained strained throughout the 1990s. Relations between Syria and Iraq improved significantly after the death of Syrian dictator Hafiz al Assad in the summer of 2000.

There have been periodic reports that Syria has provided secret financial assistance to Iraq in violation of the international sanctions. Iraq is believed to have sent $1.2 billion worth of oil to Syria through a pipeline opened in 2000. Syria—one of seven countries listed as a sponsor of terrorism in the U.S. State Department's 2002 report on global patterns of terrorism—has also been linked to clandestine efforts by Iraq to gain materials for its illegal weapons programs. After the fall of Saddam Hussein's government, the United States accused Syria of harboring high-ranking Iraqi leaders and hiding Iraqi weapons of mass destruction.

CONCLUSION

Beginning more than 5,000 years ago, the fertile land between the Tigris and Euphrates Rivers nurtured some of the world's first civilizations. In the early years of the 21st century, in the wake of Saddam Hussein's ouster, many people hoped that another major historical development would begin in Iraq: the democratization of the Middle East. That outcome is far from certain and, in any case, might take decades to come about. But whatever changes occur in the Middle East over the next few years, it is likely that Iraq—with its vast oil reserves, its large population, and its rich cultural heritage—will play an important role.

CHRONOLOGY

9000 B.C.: Earliest settlements established in the mountains of northeast Iraq.

ca. 3000 B.C.: Sumer flourishes in southern Iraq.

ca. 1750 B.C.: Hammurabi, who becomes famous for his code of laws, rules in Babylon.

1150 B.C.: Assyria conquers Babylon.

612 B.C.: The Assyrian Empire, with its capital at Nineveh in central Iraq, is conquered by Babylonian armies under Nebuchadnezzar.

539 B.C.: Babylon falls to the Persians under Cyrus the Great.

331 B.C.: The armies of Alexander the Great conquer the Persians and take control of Mesopotamia.

126 B.C.: Parthians, invaders from northern Persia, conquer Mesopotamia.

ca. A.D. 570: Muhammad, founder of the Islamic faith, is born in Mecca in the Arabian Peninsula.

636: Arabs defeat the Persians and conquer Iraq.

680: Hussein, grandson of Muhammad, is martyred in Karbala.

762: Baghdad is built as the capital of the Arab Muslim empire.

1258: Mongols capture Baghdad.

1453: Ottoman Turks conquer Constantinople, bringing an end to the Byzantine Empire.

1530: Ottoman armies conquer Baghdad and bring Mesopotamia into the Ottoman Empire.

1914: The Ottomans ally with Germany and Austria-Hungary during the First World War; British forces occupy Basra, in southern Iraq.

1917: British armies occupy Baghdad.

1918: The First World War ends.

1920: League of Nations gives British a mandate to administer Iraq.

1921: A monarchy, ruled by the Hashemite King Faisal I, is established in Iraq.

1927: Oil discovered at Kirkuk, in northern Iraq.

1932: British mandate ends, and Iraq becomes independent.

1933: King Faisal dies; his son Ghazi becomes king.

1939: King Ghazi dies in a car accident; Abdulillah rules Iraq as regent until Ghazi's infant son Faisal II is old enough to rule.

CHRONOLOGY

1953: King Faisal II crowned.

1958: Revolution takes place on July 13, and Abd al-Karim Qasim becomes the new ruler of Iraq.

1963: Qasim is killed after a coup by the Baath Party, but when Abd al-Salam Arif becomes president, he puts the Baathists out of power.

1966: Arif dies in helicopter crash; brother Abd al-Rahman Arif becomes president.

1967: Iraqi troops are sent to Jordan during the June 1967 war with Israel.

1968: After a military coup orchestrated by the Baath Party, Ahmad Hasan al-Bakr becomes president and exiles Abd al-Rahman Arif.

1969: Saddam Hussein becomes vice-chairman of the Revolutionary Command Council.

1978: The Iranian Shiite cleric Ayatollah Ruhollah Khomeini is expelled from Iraq.

1979: In July, Saddam Hussein becomes president of Iraq after a purge of the Revolutionary Command Council.

1980: In September, Iraq attacks Iran, beginning an eight-year-long war.

1988: The United Nations brokers a cease-fire to end the Iran-Iraq War.

1990: Iraq invades Kuwait, announcing that it has annexed the tiny kingdom; the international community pressures Iraq to withdraw and places sanctions on the country.

1991: An international coalition forces Iraq to withdraw from Kuwait in the brief Gulf War; the United Nations Security Council passes resolutions demanding that Iraq disarm and eliminate its programs to develop chemical, biological, and nuclear weapons.

1998: After a year of crises over the weapons inspectors, the United States launches a cruise missile attack against Iraq.

2002: George W. Bush declares Iraq part of an "axis of evil," along with Iran and North Korea; U.N. weapons inspectors return to Iraq.

2003: The U.N. pulls inspectors out of Iraq at the suggestion of the United States; the United States and Great Britain invade Iraq in March, toppling the regime of Saddam Hussein; on July 22 Saddam's sons Qusay and Uday are killed by soldiers of the U.S. Army's 101st Airborne Division.

alluvial—related to river-deposited materials like silt laid down on floodplains and deltas.

caliph—an Arabic word meaning "successor," and traditionally denoting the successor to Muhammad as head of the Islamic community.

calligraphy—artistic, elegant handwriting or lettering.

coup—the sudden, and often violent, overthrow of a government by a small group.

dialects—regional varieties of a language that are distinguished by differences in pronunciation, grammar, and vocabulary.

geometric—consisting of, or based on, shapes such as circles, squares, or straight lines.

industrialized—having many manufacturing and industrial businesses.

mandate—an order given by the League of Nations to one of its members for that member to help establish a responsible government in a former colony.

monotheistic—believing in the existence of only one God.

nationalism—the desire to achieve political independence of a people who have ethnic or cultural ties, but who do not have a state of their own.

nomadic—having no fixed home but moving from place to place.

patriarchal—relating to a social group in which the father is the supreme head, and wives and children are legally dependent upon him.

polygon—a closed figure on a sphere bounded by arcs of great circles.

plaintive—expressing suffering or woe.

regent—someone who governs a kingdom when the king is under age or is away.

salinity—the level of salt in water or soil.

secular—not religious; concerned with the present world.

shah—a Persian king or ruler.

sheikh—a term of respect and authority given to an Arab tribal leader, or to the ruler of a small kingdom called a sheikhdom.

wadi—an dry streambed that may flood after heavy rains.

FURTHER READING

Ajami, Fouad. *The Dream Palace of the Arabs: A Generation's Odyssey*. New York: Random House/Vintage Books, 1999.

Chaliand, Gerard. *A People Without a Country: The Kurds and Kurdistan*. Brooklyn, N.Y.: Olive Branch Press, 1993.

Cockburn, Andrew, and Peter Cockburn. *Out of the Ashes: The Resurrection of Saddam Hussein*. New York: HarperCollins, 1999.

Fernea, Elizabeth Warnock, and Robert A. Fernea. *The Arab World: Forty Years of Change*. New York: Bantam Doubleday Dell, 1997.

Field, Michael. *Inside the Arab World*. Cambridge, Mass.: Harvard University Press, 1995.

Hamza, Khidir, with Jeff Stein. *Saddam's Bombmaker*. New York: Simon and Schuster, 2000.

Haselkorn, Avigdor. *The Continuing Storm: Iraq, Poisonous Weapons and Deterrence*. New Haven, Conn.: Yale University Press, 1999.

Hiro, Dilip. *Neighbors, Not Friends: Iraq and Iran After the Gulf Wars*. New York: Routledge, 2001.

Hourani, Albert. *A History of the Arab Peoples*. New York: Warner Books, 1992.

Kechichian, Joseph A. *Iran, Iraq and the Arab Gulf States*. New York: St. Martin's Press, 2001.

Kremmer, Christopher. *The Carpet Wars from Kabul to Baghdad: A Ten-Year Journey Along Ancient Trade Routes*. New York: HarperCollins, 2002.

Lewis, Bernard. *The Middle East: A Brief History of the Past 2000 Years*. New York: Scribner, 1995.

———. *A Middle East Mosaic: Fragments of Life, History and Letters*. New York: Random House, 2001.

Mackey, Sandra. *The Reckoning: Iraq and the Legacy of Saddam Hussein*. New York: W. W. Norton, 2002.

Simons, Geoff. *Iraq: From Sumer to Saddam*. New York: St. Martin's Press, 1994.

Tripp, Charles. *A History of Iraq*. Cambridge, UK: Cambridge University Press, 2000.

INTERNET RESOURCES

http://usinfo.state.gov/regional/nea/iraq/

Information about Iraq, including links to informative articles, provided by the U.S. State Department.

http://www.cia.gov/cia/publications/factbook/geos/iz.html

The CIA World Factbook website provides a great deal of statistical information about Iraq and its people.

http://www.un.org/english/

The English-language web page for the United Nations can be searched for Iraq-related stories and information.

http://www.cnn.com/SPECIALS/2001/gulf.war/facts/gulfwar/

Information about the 1991 Gulf War.

http://www.theatlantic.com/issues/2002/05/bowden.htm

This profile of Saddam Hussein, originally published in *The Atlantic Monthly* in May 2002, gives details about his rule and everyday life.

INDEX

Numbers in **bold italic** refer to captions.

INDEX

PICTURE CREDITS

CONTRIBUTORS

The **FOREIGN POLICY RESEARCH INSTITUTE (FPRI)** served as editorial consultants for the MODERN MIDDLE EAST NATIONS series. FPRI is one of the nation's oldest "think tanks." The Institute's Middle East Program focuses on Gulf security, monitors the Arab-Israeli peace process, and sponsors an annual conference for teachers on the Middle East, plus periodic briefings on key developments in the region.

Among the FPRI's trustees is a former Secretary of State and a former Secretary of the Navy (and among the FPRI's former trustees and interns, two current Undersecretaries of Defense), not to mention two university presidents emeritus, a foundation president, and several active or retired corporate CEOs.

The scholars of FPRI include a former aide to three U.S. Secretaries of State, a Pulitzer Prize–winning historian, a former president of Swarthmore College and a Bancroft Prize–winning historian, and two former staff members of the National Security Council. And the FPRI counts among its extended network of scholars—especially its Inter-University Study Groups—representatives of diverse disciplines, including political science, history, economics, law, management, religion, sociology, and psychology.

DR. HARVEY SICHERMAN is president and director of the Foreign Policy Research Institute in Philadelphia, Pennsylvania. He has extensive experience in writing, research, and analysis of U.S. foreign and national security policy, both in government and out. He served as Special Assistant to Secretary of State Alexander M. Haig Jr. and as a member of the Policy Planning Staff of Secretary of State James A. Baker III. Dr. Sicherman was also a consultant to Secretary of the Navy John F. Lehman Jr. (1982–1987) and Secretary of State George Shultz (1988).

A graduate of the University of Scranton (B.S., History, 1966), Dr. Sicherman earned his Ph.D. at the University of Pennsylvania (Political Science, 1971), where he received a Salvatori Fellowship. He is author or editor of numerous books and articles, including *America the Vulnerable: Our Military Problems and How to Fix Them* (FPRI, 2002) and *Palestinian Autonomy, Self-Government and Peace* (Westview Press, 1993). He edits *Peacefacts*, an FPRI bulletin that monitors the Arab-Israeli peace process.

BILL THOMPSON graduated from Boston University with a degree in education. After teaching history in public schools, Mr. Thompson earned a Master of Divinity from Colgate-Rochester and became a Presbyterian minister. He pastored in New York, New Jersey, and Florida. He and his wife, Dorcas, now live in Swarthmore, Pennsylvania. **DORCAS (BOARDMAN) THOMPSON** graduated from Wheaton College in Illinois with a bachelor's degree in history. She taught history and social studies in Massachusetts and Pennsylvania. She has served as librarian in a private school and worked as an editor for an educational publisher in Massachusetts. She was named to *Who's Who Among America's Teachers* in 1992. The Thompsons have one daughter, Rebecca Mandia, who lives in Pennsylvania with her teacher-husband, Al. Bill and Dorcas have two grandchildren, Rachel and Patrick.